Thomas Fuller is said to have remarked that Samuel Daniel carried "in his Christian and surname two holy prophets . . . so to qualify his raptures, that he abhorred all profaneness." The remarks stands as a witty delineation of Daniel's scholarly and reserved nature. However, despite a conservative manner, he contributed substantially to the literary achievements of the seventeenth century.

Professor Seronsy divides his work roughly into two periods. During the early part of his career, Daniel helped inaugurate the sonnet vogue, took the lead in attempting a closet-drama counter to the popular stage, and versified English history in a new and influential way. The second period of his art embraces a series of poems and prose criticism that point toward the development of a philosophical view of man and his place in history.

Cecil Seronsy's study of Daniel's writings shows Daniel as an important innovator in many genres. His particular concern is, through critical examination, to reveal new aspects of Daniel's poetry and to place on firm ground a literary reputation which has undergone much fluctuation.

standing of Daniel. His published articles include studies not only of Daniel but of Shakespeare, Swift, Coleridge, and Keats. Among these articles are "The Doctrine of Cyclical Recurrence and Some Related Ideas in the Works of Samuel Daniel"; "Well - Languaged Daniel Reconsidered"; and " 'Supposes' as the unifying Theme in Shakespeare's *Taming of the Shrew*." Professor Seronsy is at present engaged in preparing a book on Shakespeare.

Twayne's English Authors Series

Sylvia E. Bowman, *Editor*

INDIANA UNIVERSITY

Samuel Daniel

TEAS 49

Samuel Daniel

By CECIL SERONSY

Bloomsburg State College

Twayne Publishers, Inc. :: New York

Preface

Samuel Daniel has long had a respectful audience, as most students of English literature know. However, to the general reader he is remembered through only two or three selections of his poetry dutifully reprinted in all the anthologies. His range of literary endeavor and his excellence as a thinker and as a man of letters deserve more attention than such scant representation has provided. While his reputation has been somewhat impaired by his own occasional lapses into prosaic flatness, he has riches which need to be singled out in a full study of his work. Daniel was a man of character and good sense, a sensitive poet, a fine critic, and a sound scholar-historian. A writer with a strong sense of the past and of his own present, he also looked to the future.

My purpose in this book is to present an account of Daniel's life and work in the successive stages of his career and to provide a critical examination of his significant writings. Above all, my aim is to assess his mind and art, at the same time taking into account what has been said of him by others from his time to ours. I believe that my discussion brings into larger focus and meaning several of his works, notably the *Funeral Poem*. It may seem to some close students of Daniel that in some sections of the book I have dealt slightly with such matters as sources, both literary and philosophical. Wherever I have done so I have deferred with acknowledgment to the closer discussions of others whom I respect. Where I may seem to have enlarged upon material of this kind, I am offering my own new information and insights, often based upon new manuscript and printed sources.

No book-length study of Daniel had appeared until Mrs. Joan Rees' *Samuel Daniel: A Critical and Biographical Study* was recently published after my book had been completed. In her fine study Mrs. Rees has anticipated some of the statements and judgments I make, although her book is generally constructed along lines different from mine. I have acknowledged in the proper places those of her observations which I think bear upon my study.

I have drawn upon some of my previous writings in various publications, and I am grateful for the permission to reprint from them. These include, for the final chapter, permission from the General Editor of the *Modern Language Review* and the Modern Humanities Research Association, the Editor of *Studies in Philology,* and the President and Fellows of Harvard College. Elsewhere in the book I am grateful for permission to reprint materials from *Notes and Queries* and the Oxford University Press, *Journal of English and Germanic Philology, Philological Quarterly, Lock Haven Bulletin,* and *Modern Language Notes.* Acknowledgment is made also to The Oxford Bibliographical Society for permission to print small portions from Sellers' *Bibliography* of Daniel and to the Yale University Press to quote portions of the text from Laurence Michel's editions of *Philotas* and the *Civil Wars.*

My first study of Daniel began several years ago under the guidance of Hyder Rollins. The writing of this book was made possible through two generous gifts of time and money in 1963–64: a grant of sabbatical leave from President Harvey A. Andruss and the Trustees of Bloomsburg State College, and a grant from the Trustees of the Henry E. Huntington Library and Art Gallery, where I spent five months of study and writing. Most helpful of all have been the staunch editorial accuracy of Professor Sylvia E. Bowman and the vigilance of my typist-critic wife, Louise.

CECIL SERONSY

Bloomsburg State College

Contents

Chronology

1562   Samuel Daniel born in Somersetshire, alleged to be son of a music master.

1581   November 17, matriculated at Oxford University (*Alumni Oxonienses*); November 29, name in Oxford University Subscription Book at Magdalen Hall. Probably met then or shortly afterward John Florio, Giordano Bruno, and Robert Ashley.

1582   November 12, Daniel's signed Latin manuscript verses at Oxford to copy of Florio's *Garden of Recreation* (Bodleian Library).

1584   Beginning of friendship with and patronage from Sir Edward Dymoke, the King's Champion.

1585   Publication of translation from *The Worthy tract of Paulus Jovius*.

1585   December until September 1586, probably in France; part of the time in diplomatic service in Paris.

1590   Probably accompanied Sir Edward Dymoke to Italy and visited the poet Guarini.

1591   Publication of Sidney's *Astrophel and Stella*, accompanied by twenty-eight of Daniel's sonnets.

1592   March, living at Lincoln in the household of Dymoke. Publication of *Delia* and the *Complaint of Rosamond* (in two editions). Already under guidance and patronage of Mary, Countess of Pembroke and Fulke Greville. Perhaps just made tutor to William Herbert, Earl of Pembroke.

1593   October 19, *Cleopatra* entered in Stationers' Register. Daniel shows knowledge of the Sidney translation of the Psalms.

1593–1594   Charles Blount, Lord Mountjoy, becomes friend and patron of the poet.

1594   Publication of *Cleopatra,* together with another edition of *Delia* and *Rosamond* "augmented" and much revised. Manuscripts of Books I–III of *Civil Wars* already begun and completed.

1595   Publication of first four books of the *Civil Wars.*

1597– 1603   In household of Lady Margaret, Countess of Cumberland; tutor to her daughter, Anne Clifford.

1599   Publication of *The Poetical Essays,* containing *Civil Wars* (first five books); *Musophilus; A Letter from Octavia; The Tragedy of Cleopatra* (partly revised); *Rosamond.*

1600   Apparently in favor with Queen Elizabeth and recipient of royal patronage.

1601   *Works,* "newly augmented," containing *Civil Wars* revised and a sixth book added, and all the other poems previously published, some considerably revised.

1601– 1603   Likely encouragement and patronage from Sir Thomas Egerton.

1603   April, presentation to the incoming King James of *A Panegyrike Congratulatorie,* with publication shortly thereafter. Publication of six new verse epistles and *A Defence of Ryme,* along with some earlier writings.

1604   Made licenser for the Children of the Queen's Revels (probably through the influence of the Countess of Bedford) until April 28, 1605. Won patronage of the Earl of Hertford. Presented at Hampton Court the masque, *The Vision of the Twelve Goddesses,* and shortly thereafter published it. Possibly staged a performance of the tragedy *Philotas.*

1605   Publication of *Certaine Small Poems* (most of them issued before) and the *Tragedie of Philotas.* Letters written to Lord Cranbourne and Earl of Devonshire, seeking to exculpate Daniel from any charge of political intent in writing *Philotas.*

     August, presentation of the pastoral drama *The Queens Arcadia* to the Queen, at Christ Church, Oxford.

1606   Publication of the *Funeral Poem* on death of the Earl of Devonshire (Mountjoy).

1607   Publication of *Certaine Small Workes,* all previously published but again much revised. Daniel designated as gentleman extraordinary and one of the grooms of the privy chamber to Anne, Queen Consort of James I, a post he held until his death in 1619.

1608   May, two letters from Daniel to James Kirton, officer in the Earl of Hertford's household, indicating residence on a farm, possibly in Wiltshire, and in the process of undertaking important business in London.

1609   Final publication of the *Civil Wars* in eight books (much expanded and revised).

1610   June 5, the masque *Tethys Festival* "celebrated" at Whitehall. Publication of *Tethys Festival*.

1612   *First Part of the Historie of England,* dedicated to Sir Robert Carr, Lord Roxborough.

1614   February 3, presentation of *Hymen's Triumph,* to celebrate nuptials of Lord Roxborough at Somerset House, on the Strand.

1615   Publication of *Hymen's Triumph.* Grant of permission from Office of Revels to manage a company of youths to perform comedies and tragedies at Bristol.

1618   Publication of *The Collection of the History of England.* June, the Revels office at Bristol transferred to Daniel's brother. June, July, indications of the poet's illness.

1619   September 4, last will made; died at Beckington, near Phipps Norton, in Somersetshire, where he had retired to a farm at Rudge some years earlier. October 14, burial in Beckington churchyard.

1623   *Whole Works,* published by brother John, containing all the works of Daniel in verse.

CHAPTER 1

The Beginnings (1562-1593)

THE generation into which Samuel Daniel was born was destined to be the most fruitful in the history of English poetry. But the promise in 1562 of the new poetry to come seems in the twentieth century to fall far short of the event. Chaucer remained the dominating figure to whom writers continued to point with national pride. The courtly makers of Henry VIII's time, notably Sir Thomas Wyatt and the Earl of Surrey, had not only introduced the sonnet into England but had also accommodated that form to the English idiom. Wyatt enriched the new English poetry with a vigor and earnest intensity; and Surrey, in creating a native sonnet form later to be known as "Shakespearian," gave to it a smoothness of versification. Some forty years were to pass before lyrical poetry was to go very far beyond this point. However, the intervening years were not altogether fallow because numerous verse anthologies, such as Richard Tottel's in 1554, helped to nourish the tradition of poetry to which George Turberville and George Gascoigne a decade or so later made valuable contributions. Moreover, the tremendous interest in the moral value of history was reflected in *The Mirror for Magistrates* (1559)—a book that was to profoundly influence later English poetry and drama.

Daniel was a few years younger than Spenser, Sidney, and Ralegh; and he was almost the same age as Marlowe, Shakespeare, Drayton, and Sir John Harington—to name only a few of his contemporaries who later contributed to the great outburst of poetry in the 1580's and 1590's. And Daniel's share in that achievement, particularly as an exemplary influence, was no small one.

I *Family, College, and Early Writing*

He was born in Somersetshire in the year 1562, and though no evidence has been found to support the statement of Thomas Fuller and others after him that Daniel's father was a master of music, Fuller's additional comment has interest: "his harmonious mind made an impression on his son's genius, who proved an exquisite poet." [1] Daniel's younger brother John, however, was a musician and composer of some note. Samuel Daniel appears throughout his career as a quiet, serious, almost shy man of letters; and, as will be seen, these qualities are manifested very early —indeed, we might say they are prefigured in his very birth and naming. As Fuller wittily observes, "He carried in his Christian and surname two holy prophets . . . so to qualify his raptures, that he abhorred all profaneness." It is just possible too that his name has frightened off a certain class of modern readers.

Of Daniel's boyhood nothing is known. At nineteen he entered Magdalen College, Oxford University, where he matriculated on November 17, 1581. [2] There he met John Florio, remembered today mainly for his later translation of Montaigne. Many biographers of Daniel and Florio assume without much evidence that the two men were later brothers-in-law and build interesting inferences from this assumption. At any rate, scholars are certain that Florio, destined to be Daniel's lifelong friend, taught Italian at Oxford, where November 12, 1582, he dedicated his manuscript volume *Giardino di recreatione* to Edward Dyer. This collection of proverbs, containing four Latin verses by Daniel that make puns on Florio's name, are Daniel's earliest recorded verses. Other lines in this manuscript are by their fellow collegian Matthew Gwinne, who later contributed verses, usually signed "Il Candido," to many of Florio's published works. It is interesting to note that the writings of these three young Oxford men of the 1580's are found together again almost a quarter of a century later in another and more famous undertaking, Florio's translation of Montaigne's *Essays* (1603); Daniel wrote for it some eloquent verses on both the author and the translator; Gwinne prefixed a sonnet on Lady Rich that practically identified her with the Stella of Sidney's sonnets.

During Daniel's three-year stay at Oxford he in all probability met the great Italian humanist and philosopher Giordano Bruno, who came to lecture at the university in 1583, perhaps at Florio's suggestion. Despite the contrast between Bruno's vehemence and Daniel's calm, it has been suggested that the Italian's *Eroici Fur-*

ori may have influenced some of Daniel's later work.[3] He is clearly the "Nolanus" referred to in "N. W.'s" epistle to Daniel in the latter's *Paulus Jovius,* a book which was soon to appear in 1585. Daniel was probably well acquainted too with Robert Ashley, a student and later fellow at Magdalen in the early 1580's. Ashley in the course of his life translated six works from the Italian, French, and Spanish languages; and one of these is a translation from the French of Le Roy in 1594, which Daniel no doubt read, perhaps both in the original and in translation, and which apparently influenced his own conception of historical change.

These early associations of Daniel with Florio, Gwinne, Bruno, and Ashley suggest an interest in languages and translation; and we are not surprised to find that Daniel's first published work is a translation from the Italian of a well-known book. The title page reads, in part, "The Worthy tract of Paulus Jovius, contayning a Discourse of rare inventions, both Militarie and Amorous *called Imprese.* Whereunto is added a Preface contayning the arte of composing them, with many other notable devises. By Samuell Daniell late student in Oxenforde." Apparently, he had left Oxford without a degree. The publisher of this translation, Simon Waterson, henceforth undertook to publish nearly all of Daniel's subsequent work, and he remained a faithful friend throughout the poet's lifetime.

Several circumstances connected with this first book need to be mentioned since they suggest certain traits and patterns which can be recognized throughout Daniel's career. Modern scholars and critics, in their haste to dismiss him as prosaic and too much the poet of statement, have tended to ignore the fact that he was an innovator. And, though perhaps not original in the highest sense, he was yet a "first" in many important ways. The literature on emblems had become extensive in Italy in the sixteenth century, and the interest in them grew rapidly in England late in that century and into the next. Sidney's letters from Italy show that he was reading books on imprese, among them the *Worthy Tract* in its original Italian.[4] The interest in emblems is found in Edmund Spenser (*Shepherd's Calendar* particularly), John Donne, George Herbert, Francis Quarles, and others. Abraham Fraunce wrote a treatise on the subject in 1582. Before any book on emblems had been published in England, Daniel made his translation; presented a clear, concise account of the subject; and added new material of his own.

Daniel's Preface "To the Friendly Reader," distinguishes between *Impreses* and other *Devises,* on the ground that an *Impresa* denotes a particular enterprise with a particular end in view, one which can be signified by "some figure & mot" that is usually worn on standards, shields, and brooches. The "mot or posie" should be a quotation from a famous author, should not ordinarily exceed three words, and should avoid both the obvious and the obscure. Both the "mot" and the figure signified are required to give the intended meaning.[5] Then follows Daniel's full translation, in the form of a dialogue between Paulus Jovius, Bishop of Nocera, and Ludovicus Dominicus. Following this is an account of Daniel's own collection of "certaine noble devises, both militarie and amorous," several of them being described in racy, narrative manner, suggestive of the Italian *novella.*

Just before Daniel's own Preface is an Epistle to him from 'N.W.' that is dated from Oxford on November 20 and that urges an apparently reluctant Daniel to publish this translation. This Oxford friend uncovers in colorful style some of Daniel's qualities: "You blush to open another man's shop and sell *Italian* wares as though you were a Bankerupt in philosophie." He rightly commends Daniel's nakedness of style though he notes that Daniel is troubled about it; and he then proceeds to bolster the poet's faint spirit from time to time, as when he asks, "What neede you then to feare the mallice of the weakest enemy that may bee a carping tongue?" [6] Thus early from the unknown "N.W." comes this remarkably clear intimation of Daniel's temper and personality.

II   *Travel and Early Patronage*

And the *Worthy Tract* provides one more hint of what is to come. The book is dedicated to Sir Edward Dymoke (hereditary king's champion and apparently already a friend and patron of Daniel) as "a present of the first fruites" of the writer's work. Dymoke was the first of a long line of noble and royal patrons who gave Daniel the help and encouragement he needed: Mary, Countess of Pembroke; Fulke Greville; Lord Mountjoy; the Countess of Cumberland; the Countess of Bedford; Sir Thomas Egerton; Queen Elizabeth; Queen Anne; King James; the Earl of

Hertford; the Earl of Pembroke; and Viscount Carr. In an age when the patronage of the great was sought for with varying success by most men of letters, as the experience of Spenser shows, such a list as this, by any count, is an impressive one. If we wonder how such a shy, retiring person as Daniel managed so well with his patrons, the answer is to be found perhaps in the tact and moderation—he is never effusive in his praise—which he shows throughout his career, with perhaps one or two notable exceptions.

Shortly after the publication of his first book, Daniel spent some of his next five years traveling in France and in Italy. It has not been fully proved that he made these journeys, but the evidence is strong for supposing that he did. Two letters from Paris by a Samuel Daniel indicate that he was in France in December, 1585, and that he secured in the following spring diplomatic employment with the English ambassador at Paris, Sir Edward Stafford. Daniel was entrusted with dispatches which he delivered on his return to England to Walsingham at Windsor Castle on September 7, 1586.[7] The likelihood of visits to France and Italy by an impressionable young man of poetic temperament is important to understanding his development. French influence is very strong in the early work of Daniel, particularly in the sonnets and in the drama; and the Italian influence began early and continued into his later writing. Probably the young man was stimulated by direct association and conversation with his French and Italian literary contemporaries. Moreover, his own word on his foreign travels in the dedicatory Epistle to his later *History* (1612) reveals that he has spent much time in humane learning "both in forraine countries, where especially I took these notions" (about history) and also at home.[8]

Reminiscences of an Italian visit are also found at various places in Daniel's writings. He must have visited Italy with his patron Dymoke in 1590 or shortly thereafter. His dedicatory sonnet addressed to Dymoke and prefixed to the anonymous English translation of Guarini's *Pastor Fido* in 1602 refers to such a visit and to an extensive association with Guarini:

> Though I remember he hath oft imbas'd
> Unto us both the vertues of the North,

> Saying, our costes were with no measures grac'd,
> Nor barbarous tongues could any verse bring forth.
> I would he saw his owne, or knew our store,
> Whose spirits can yeeld as much, and if not more.

The early editions of Daniel's *Civil Wars* (1595) have some lines suggesting an intimacy with and affection for Lombardy, where Guarini lived:

> For as the spreading members of proud *Po,*
> That thousand-branched *Po,* whose limmes embrace
> The fertile and delicious body so
> Sweet *Lombardie,* and beautifies thy face.[9]

Along with the sweet recollections of the South, however, is the sturdy defense of England's merits, evident in the lines to Dymoke above and a theme to which Daniel returns many times. The imputation of the inferiority of English as a language and as a literature haunts him throughout his career, and it is as though he feels he must reply to Guarini again and again. Thus, in the 1594 dedication to his tragedy of *Cleopatra,* Daniel wants to be certain "That they might know how far *Thames* doth out-go/ The Musike of declined *Italy.*" And in 1599 he returns to the theme in *Musophilus* (955–56): "When all that ever hotter spirits exprest/ Comes bettered by the patience of the North." Even as late as 1607 in another dedication to *Cleopatra,* in which he ranks Sidney above all modern authors, Daniel once more reminds his reader "That they might know how far Thames doth out goe/ Declined Tyber." Daniel holds in high esteem French and Italian literature, but he is an Englishman to the core. He had translated Paulus Jovius and later imitated Guarini on more than one occasion, yet he was sure that the future of poetry lay in the North.

The Italian journey is referred to in sonnet forty-four of the 1592 edition of *Delia* and in forty-seven of the 1594 edition. The latter bears the note "At the authors going into Italie," [10] but we cannot be certain of the date of the visit. At any rate, Daniel must have been back in England at least by late 1591, for he was living in Dymoke's household at Lincoln in March, 1592, where at one point he was himself involved in a long series of family quarrels and litigation that occasionally had comic overtones.[11] Both Sir

Edward Dymoke and his witty mercurial brother Tailboys, himself prankster and poet, had developed a strong hostility toward their irascible uncle, the Earl of Lincoln, who suffered from a sense of persecution and against whom Tailboys devised a Maygames play. Tailboys, among other satirical pieces, later wrote a comic allegorical poem, *Caltha Poetorum* (The Marigold of the Poets), published in 1599, which still remains pretty much a puzzle. Daniel—and of course this is the Daniel of the later 1590's—is referred to in the Preface as "Pollished *Daniel* the Historick"; and in the poem proper he may possibly be, as Leslie Hotson suggests, the *Musaeus* into which Diana transforms the bee and which then entertains the ladies of the court.

But these events and references come at a much later time than the spring days in 1592 when Daniel was living in Lincoln. Edward Dymoke wrote on March 1 a letter to Lord Lincoln's son setting forth the Earl's intolerable, unjust behavior that was likely to have dire consequences. Dymoke, wisely dissuaded from sending this threatening letter, gave it to his servant Samuel Daniel to be burnt. But the ever cautious Daniel, true to his characteristic temperance, put the letter into a hole in the wall of Dymoke's house. Four years later the house was sold to the Earl of Lincoln, who in pulling down the wall for repairs eventually found the letter. The raging Earl now started legal action that did not end until 1610 with the imposition of a very heavy fine on Sir Edward Dymoke,[12] who must have often had bitter reflections about Daniel's caution.

We cannot resist speculating about the impact of the effervescent Tailboys, whom Hotson sees as a kind of Mercutio, upon Daniel, who, now thirty years old, was writing sonnets and composing his narrative love-poem *The Complaint of Rosamond*. Was Daniel encouraged to tarry briefly among "loves soft lays and looser thoughts delight," in Spenser's phrase, before moving on to the tragedy and the epic of more serious intent? We would like to know more about this early association of two poets so markedly unlike in temperament.

The publication of John Florio's *Second Fruits* in 1591 indicates that he and Daniel were still closely associated. This collection in Italian and English of dialogues containing proverbial matter bears a prefatory sonnet from "Phäeton to his friend Florio." The style and matter of the poem suggest that "Phäeton" may be Daniel, who may also be the shy and thoughtful person whom Florio introduces into the sixth dialogue as, the "Daniel" walking "solitarie along the streete." One of the other characters remarks that he "does ever goe with his head downeward, as you see him now." When modest "Daniel" enters, Nicholas, who in some ways reminds us of Florio, remarks: "As each flower from the sonne, so I receave vertue and force from your presence." And "Daniel" answers: "And as each river to the sea, so do I run to offer myself unto you." [13] These words closely parallel the opening lines of Daniel's first sonnet, published for the first time in 1592; and the suggestion is strong that some of his sonnets in manuscript were in circulation among his friends considerably before this date. The tone of friendly parody is what might be expected of Florio.

III   *The Countess of Pembroke and Wilton*

By 1592, perhaps earlier, Daniel had found in Mary, Countess of Pembroke, the help, the guidance, and the encouragement that was to launch him upon his literary career. Her brother Sir Philip Sidney in the late 1570's had gathered round himself poets with such diverse talents as Fulke Greville and Edward Dyer, and by his own example and encouragement had opened a way for the new English poetry that was to be at flood tide in another decade. Sidney not only wrote the great prose romance *Arcadia*, rich in plot, dramatic structure, and characterization, as well as in poetry, but also encouraged and helped direct Spenser in creating his great English epic poem, *The Faerie Queene*. Sidney's sonnet sequence *Astrophel and Stella*, through its varied experimentation in verse and in its note of intense personal feeling, established firmly the sonneteering vogue that lasted through the remainder of the century. Finally his *Defence of Poesie*, which surely was a model from which Daniel worked in his own *Defence of Ryme*, established the rank and dignity of poetry and England's place in the tradition; and it remains one of the greatest documents in English literary criticism. In 1580 Sidney, temporarily out of favor at court, came to Wilton to reside with his sister. There he composed the *Arcadia* and began the translation of the Holy Psalms into English—a work his sister later completed. Sidney left England for the last time in 1585 and died from wounds received in the

Battle of Zutphen the following year. Although Daniel expresses a deep veneration for him as man and poet, there is no evidence that they ever met.

Mary Sidney's life span (1561–1621) almost exactly parallels Daniel's. After spending most of her girlhood at court, she married Henry Herbert, the second Earl of Pembroke in April, 1577, the year she came to Wilton. She must have passed the greater part of her married life there until 1601, when on the death of her husband she became the Countess Dowager of Pembroke. Of her four children the eldest, William, born in 1580, is particularly noteworthy. Daniel probably succeeded Hugh (or Henry) Sanford as tutor to this boy; and in 1603, after William had become the third Earl of Pembroke, the poet addressed to his former pupil the *Defence of Rhyme*. And, of course, he is the William Herbert whose name is linked with Shakespeare's and one of the two brothers to whom the 1623 Folio of Shakespeare was dedicated.

The Countess of Pembroke in her own day was famed as a favorer of learning and as a friend of poets. At her death she was remembered as "Sidney's sister, Pembroke's mother" and as "the subject of all verse." The poets who gathered about her in the earlier years at Wilton were not writing for the popular stage; and the few, like Daniel and Greville, who did write tragedies, wrote closet dramas of the Classical Senecan type in which the countess and her circle were interested. She seems to have been most generous and encouraging to many of these nondramatic poets. To her were addressed dedications and commendatory poems from Nicholas Breton, Thomas Howell, Abraham Fraunce, Thomas Watson, Barnaby Barnes, Thomas Morley, John Davies of Hereford, John Donne, Spenser, Daniel, Drayton, and others. John Aubrey, who is not always a reliable authority, is probably close to the truth when he says in his *Brief Lives* that "In her time Wilton House was like a college, there were so many learned and ingeniose persons. She was the greatest patronesse of witt and learning of any lady in her time." [14]

It was into this Wilton household that Daniel came some time during or after his foreign visits. We don't know how he first attracted the notice of the countess, but it has been suggested that his friend Florio introduced him to her, for she would have been interested in the translation of Paulus Jovius which her brother knew in Italian.[15] Or Daniel may have come as a tutor either to assist or to succeed Sanford. However that may be, the poet became a kind of pupil himself under the able direction of the countess. He tells us so in the *Defence of Ryme* addressed to her own son many years later, in 1603, when speaking of his early poetry: "Having beene first incourag'd or fram'd thereunto by your most Worthy and Honourable Mother, receiving the first notion for the formall ordering of those compositions at *Wilton,* which I must ever acknowledge to have beene my best Schoole, and therof alwayes am to hold a feeling and gratefull Memory." [16]

We might hazard a guess that in the very early 1590's Daniel was much interested in the Countess of Pembroke's continued translation of the Psalms that Sidney had carried through number forty-three. Her own versions show a great variety of verse forms, and her poems are often superior to those of her brother.[17] The countess must have undertaken to complete Sidney's translation several years after his death in 1586 since the earliest printed reference to her work comes from Daniel in the prefatory lines to *Cleopatra,* probably written earlier than October, 1593, when the play was entered on the Stationers' Register. Possibly she began the continuation of the Psalms shortly after completing her translation of Garnier's *Antonie* from the French in 1590, not long before Daniel himself came to Wilton. No doubt the poet spent a great deal of time with the countess, who frequently revised and polished not only her own but her brother's psalms until she completed the whole, probably in 1599,[18] though it remained in manuscript form for two centuries after her death.

Daniel was already beginning to revise and tinker with his own earlier poetry in 1592 and 1593, so it would seem that opportunities were abundant for his discussing with the countess their exercises and problems in versification. At any rate, the success of her undertaking was on his mind in 1594 when he pays homage in his Preface to *Cleopatra* for her accomplishment:

> Those *Hymnes* that thou doost consecrate to heaven,
> Which *Israel's* Singer to his God did frame
> Unto thy voyce eternitie hath given,
> And makes thee deere to him from whence they came
> In them must rest thy ever reverent name,
> So long as *Syons* God remaineth honoured.

Although probably never intended for publication, these poems, in Daniel's opinion, merited eternal fame. His view expresses a faith current in a day when manuscripts were circulated among friends and when at least some poets were reluctant to get into print.

Some readers of Daniel must have often thought that he was himself a collaborator in the translation of the Psalms because of the presence of what has seemed a curious poem, "To the Angell spirit of the Most excellent Sir Phillip Sidney," which first appeared in the posthumous collection of Daniel's works in verse and in later editions. If we assume that the poem is his, its wording suggests his part in a dual authorship. But the attribution of "To the Angell spirit" to Daniel was early suspected by Coleridge.[19] And more recently a manuscript of the Psalms has been found bearing the "Daniel" poem and, following it, these words: "by the Sister of that Incomparable Sidney." [20]

Thus the lines, not Daniel's at all, somehow got into the 1623 edition by mistake. Since the printed version of "To the Angell spirit" appears to be earlier than the recently discovered manuscript version, especially noticeable in its uncompleted final stanza, it was probably derived from an earlier manuscript copy which remained among Daniel's possessions from the Wilton days until his death in 1619. This story of mistaken authorship is certainly a consequence of the poet's close associations with the countess at Wilton in the early 1590's. Such was the favorable environment into which Daniel had moved, and it was from this vantage point that he was in the next half decade to first launch a body of poetry that established his influence and reputation.

CHAPTER 2

Early Poetry: Sonnet and Narrative
(1590-1592)

I *The Delia Sonnets*

DANIEL'S first poems appeared in print in 1591 and were linked advantageously with the name of Sir Philip Sidney, who had died five years before. The occasion was an unauthorized edition by the publisher Thomas Newman of Sidney's *Astrophel and Stella,* together with "sundry other rare Sonnets," including twenty-eight by Daniel, who had possibly already been circulating his poems in manuscript among friends. In the following year Daniel brought out his own version of the sonnets under the title *Delia* and, along with them, a narrative poem *The Complaint of Rosamond.* The 1592 edition contained a total of fifty sonnets, including twenty-three that were carefully revised from Newman's edition. The prose dedication to Mary, Countess of Pembroke, sets forth Daniel's reason for publication: "Although I rather desired to keep in the private passions of my youth, from the multitude, as things utterd by myselfe, and consecrated to silence: yet seeing I was betraide by the indiscretion of a greedie Printer, and had some of my secrets bewraide to the world, uncorrected: doubting the like of the rest, I am forced to publish that which I never ment." [1]

This reluctance to publish, a convention among Elizabethan writers, need not detain us. The point is that Daniel's name was auspiciously linked with Sidney's from the start and that in 1592 he made haste to "correct" Newman's text. Thereafter he corrected, revised, and added to the sonnets, as was his practice with most of his later work. He was an inveterate reviser, as may be seen from the changes he made to *Delia* alone. A second edition followed in the same year, 1592, with four new sonnets. In 1594 appeared fifty-five sonnets: five of them, new; eighteen of them, revised. Slight changes were made in the editions of 1595 and

1598, and the most thoroughgoing alterations of all appeared in 1601.

Daniel's sonnets are unlike Sidney's in form. Sidney experimented in a wide variety of rhymes and in the metrical length of his lines; in general, the form is Italian, with octave and sestet clearly marked. Daniel's sonnet is predominantly "Elizabethan" or "Shakespearian" with three unlinked quatrains, followed by a couplet. In form, at least, Shakespeare is closer to Daniel than to Sidney or to Spenser. It has been amply demonstrated that Daniel had not only studied French and Italian models closely, but had also in some instances paraphrased in part the sonnets of Tasso, Du Bellay, and particularly Desportes. The French influence, itself derived from Italian, is the more direct. On the whole, comparison of Daniel's sonnets with their foreign sources shows that he emerges with original work, with poems that can be called his own.[2]

Such conventional themes embodied in the sonnet form as the sleeplessness of the lover, as in Daniel's "Care-charmer sleepe"; of absence; of wasting in despair; of beauty that must fade; and the many conceits of the heart and of the mirror—all these and many more were the common stock of sonneteers as far back as Petrarch. So it can be truly said that poets borrowed freely from one another, and often our surprise at discovering this fact seems a little naïve. Moreover, there is also the question of the author's intention. In applying established conceits to the person addressed in the sonnets was the poet always being "sincere"? Are we to accept literally all that is said of Sidney's Stella and of Daniel's Delia? And who is Delia? Much of Stella as a real person can be accepted, though not all. Delia, however, is more shadowy; and her identification with the Countess of Pembroke or anyone else is tenuous, if not wholly unacceptable.

The occasionally passionate but more often despairing attitude of the poet toward Delia does not seem to be the tone Daniel would adopt toward his patroness. The strongest argument against the identification is the presence in the second 1592 edition of sonnet thirty-nine addressed to "M.P." If we assume that "M.P." stands for Mary Pembroke, it seems unlikely that one sonnet should be so designated if the whole sequence is likewise addressed to her. But one editor goes further and rejects identification in even this sonnet on the questionable ground that it is unlikely a dependent would be so bold as to use these simple initials.[3] The argument that this sonnet *is* addressed to the countess and that she is not Delia finds strong support in an examination of the poet's successive revisions. First there appeared the prose dedication to the Countess of Pembroke in both editions of 1592. After that date there was probably no further need for the poet's explanation of how he came to publish *Delia*, and the dedication was dropped. But the second edition of 1592 contained the "M.P." sonnet, the only one within the cycle in which there is no trace of a lover's passion. Instead, the poet expresses his want and distress, but he does not explicitly address anyone for help. After 1592, the sonnet was omitted, but in the next edition of 1594 the prose dedication was replaced by a dedicatory sonnet to the Countess of Pembroke, fervently praising her kindness and favor. Like the sonnet to "M.P.", there is nothing amatory about the poem; it merely suggests that the poet's want has been relieved. Now with the 1594 sonnets appeared *Cleopatra*, entered in the Stationers' Register on October 19, 1593. This tragedy was written under the kindly influence of the countess, as Daniel himself acknowledges in the opening lines of his dedication to her:

> Shee, whose cleere brightnes doth alone infuse
> Strength to my thoughts, and makes mee what I am;
> Call'd up my spirits from out their low repose,
> To sing of state, and tragick notes to frame.
>
> I, who (contented with an humble song,)
> Made musique to myselfe that pleas'd mee best,
> And onely told of D E L I A, and her wrong,
> And prais'd her eyes, and plain'd mine owne unrest.[4]

These lines further indicate that the Countess of Pembroke had no very close connection with the substance of the Delia sonnets. And the fact that this dedication and the 1594 sonnet of thanks are Daniel's earliest explicit acknowledgments of gratitude to the countess suggests that the poet did not receive material assistance from her until later than has been supposed, perhaps late in 1592.

It seems clear that he was writing sonnets before he came to Wilton, and probably before 1590.

The 1592 sonnets have a progression, a thread that links many of them in phrasing and theme. But they have no real dramatic progression whatever; throughout is a seeming involvement with a woman, accompanied by a languid, unrequited love. There are no climaxes, no suggestions of a personal encounter, of parting, or of reconciliation, as in Shakespeare and Sidney. An example of this uncertainty is the second sonnet, beginning

> Goe wailing verse, the infants of my love
> *Minerva*-like brought foorth without a Mother:
> Present the image of the cares I prove,
> Witnes your Fathers griefe exceedes all other.

The tone suggests a Delia somewhere between a real person and the object of a poetical exercise. The vain pursuit of a disdainful maid, whatever her identity, is the theme running through the whole. Whatever the tone and theme, however, the new poet displays unusual qualities in his art.

Daniel often strikes a characteristically quiet note, pure in diction and limpid in imagery. Thus in the fourth sonnet Apollo is addressed:

> No Bayes I seeke to deck my mourning brow,
> O cleer-eyde Rector of the holie Hill:
> My humble accents crave the Olyve bow,
> Of her milde pittie and relenting will.

The same note is sounded again in the sixth sonnet, to the accompaniment of a lovely slow-moving monosyllabic line: "A modest maide, deckt with a blush of honour,/ Whose feete doe treade greene pathes of youth and love."

Daniel is most effective in his use of the submerged mythological allusion in which, with little explicit reference, the myth is ingeniously applied to the poet's own situation—as in the Actaeon myth in the fifth sonnet:

> Whilst youth and error led my wandring minde,
> And set my thoughts in heedeles waies to range:

All unawares a Goddesse chaste I finde,
Diana-like, to worke my suddaine change.
    For her no sooner had my view bewrayd,
But with disdaine to see me in that place:
With fairest hand, the sweet unkindest maide,
Castes water-cold disdaine upon my face.
    Which turn'd my sport into a Harts dispaire,
Which still is chac'd, whilst I have any breath,
By mine owne thoughts: set on me by my faire,
My thoughts like houndes, pursue me to my death.
    Those that I fostred of mine owne accord,
    Are made by her to murther thus their Lord.

In the ninth sonnet Daniel achieves a masterpiece of compression in his quiet evocation of Sisyphus: "The never-resting stone of care to roule." The presence of Cupid is no more than noticed in the opening of the twelfth sonnet, and he is kept at exactly the proper distance: "My spotles love hoovers with white wings,/ About the temple of the proudest frame." Sonnets twenty-seven and twenty-eight apply to the poet's own defeated aspirations the resources of the Icarus myth; in fact, the 1594 edition contained an additional sonnet embodying this myth, thus extending it through three consecutive sonnets.

Daniel is able to impart a unity to his whole sequence in a number of ways: by the presence of Delia throughout; by the persistent if somewhat undramatic theme of the wailing, despairing lover meeting with disdain; and by the use of devices for linking the sonnets together to give them the effect of continuity, of organic life. Just as sometimes a single theme, like the Icarus myth cited above, may spill over from one sonnet into another, so the whole of a last line, or a phrase from it, in one sonnet is taken up at the beginning of the one that follows. Such linking occurs in sonnets twenty-four and twenty-five, twenty-seven and twenty-eight, thirty-two through thirty-five, and forty-two and forty-three. Hence, although the dramatic thrust and close personal note may be lacking in *Delia*, the outer structural devices employed show a conscious, skilled artistry at work in building toward a whole. Within the individual sonnets themselves a close relationship between the structural parts is usually attained, as in the fourteenth sonnet, "Those amber locks,"; by no means one of the best in the sequence, Daniel nevertheless skillfully develops in it corresponding sets of objects and images in three's and gathers them along the way toward the hoped-for restoration of the lover in the final line.

The theme of *carpe diem* is often resorted to in the sequence. Sonnet thirty, beginning "I once may see when yeeres shall wreck my wronge," looks ahead to the time when Delia, now old, gray, and wrinkled, "must yeelde up all to tyrant Times desire" and, as she looks in her glass, must then be reminded of what she once was by the poet's verses, whose "firie heate" shall make her, like the Phoenix, live anew. The conventional devices do not prevent this sonnet from being finely executed. Nevertheless, while the workmanship is there, and while the tone is sweet and restrained, the poem, typically, never quite succeeds. Daniel too seldom soars or attains the thrilling phrase that transfigures poetry.

The same theme of *carpe diem* occurs in the lovely thirty-first sonnet beginning "Looke *Delia* how we steeme the half-blowne Rose,/ The image of thy blush and Summers honor," and again in sonnet thirty-two, "And *Delia,* thinke thy morning must have night/ And that thy brightnes sets at length to west." One fine sonnet that at the close falls sharply off is the forty-second, which opens with the lovely line, "Beautie, sweet love, is like the morning dewe." It develops through its imagery the frailty and evanescence of this beauty, and rises to a majesty and power reminiscent of Shakespeare:

> When thou surcharg'd with burthen of thy yeeres,
> Shalt bend thy wrinkles homeward to the earth:
> When tyme hath made a pasport for thy feares,
> Dated in age the Kalends of our death.

A beautifully sustained sonnet, it culminates in this magnificently slow-measured passage. Only two lines remain, but in them the grand style is not sustained; for the poet drops into the moralizing tone of a disillusioned old woman: "But ah no more, thys hath beene often tolde,/ And women grieve to thinke they must be old." The poem descends too abruptly into literal application, and much of the magic is lost.

Daniel's most famous sonnet is the forty-fifth, the one piece of his which everyone has read—"Care-charmer sleepe, sonne of the Sable night." Certainly one of its most telling features is its fluidity of movement, its rising and falling tone, its swift juxtaposition of the images of night and day—all suggesting the troubled state of mind in the lover caught between two worlds, neither of which, we feel certain, he can wholly attain. Daniel has captured perfectly the tension between the quiet rest of night and the cruel, cold turbulence of day.

The sonnet immediately following this last is, except for its rapid descent into flatness in the final couplet, equally great:

> Let others sing of Knights and Palladines,
> In aged accents, and untimely words:
> Paint shadowes in imaginary lines,
> Which well the reach of their high wits records;
> But I must sing of thee and those faire eyes,
> Autentique shall my verse in time to come,
> When yet th'unborne shall say, loe where she lyes,
> Whose beautie made him speake that els was dombe.
> These are the Arkes the Tropheis I erect,
> That fortifie thy name against old age,
> And these thy sacred vertues must protect,
> Against the Darke and times consuming rage.
> Though th'error of my youth they shall discover,
> Suffice they shew I liv'd and was thy lover.

In this sonnet the poet first gracefully pays tribute to those poets who, like Spenser, have the gift for high romance; and then he moves on in the second quatrain to the eternizing mood of the Shakespeare sonnets. Certainly the line "Against the Darke and times consuming rage" presages Shakespeare's "Not marble, nor the gilded monuments." The whole is in the best tradition of Elizabethan sonnetry.

II *Influence of the Sonnets*

But how extensive a shaping force were Daniel's sonnets upon his contemporaries? He exerted some influence upon the work of Richard Barnfield as well as Bartholomew Griffin, two of whose sonnets, "Care-charmer, sleep" and "Fair is my love," obviously echo Daniel's forty-fifth and forty-sixth sonnets, respectively. A

more important imitator was Michael Drayton, who was also influenced by Daniel in other areas of poetry. Drayton's varied poetical career extended through the reigns of Elizabeth, James I, and
Charles I. He became a page at Polesworth, in the house of Sir
Henry Goodere, whose daughter Anne became the "Idea" of his
sonnets; long after she married, Drayton remained a devoted
friend to her. Himself not university-educated, this fervid enthusi-
astic poet whose Renaissance English enthusiasm was later to find
its fullest expression in the great topographical poem *Polyolbion*
(1612, 1622) began with Daniel as a guide, first in his sonnets—
Ideas Mirrour (1595) that he later revised thoroughly in the more
concentrated, more conversational shape of Donne's and Sidney's
verse; then in his several narrative, erotic poems modeled after
Daniel's *Rosamond;* and finally in his historical poems which bear
influences of Daniel's treatment of English history. As early as
1593, in the sixth eclogue of *Idea, The Shepheards Garland,* he
has extravagant praise for Mary, Countess of Pembroke, whom he
calls "Minerva," as does Daniel in his second sonnet. It is doubtful, however, that Drayton ever enjoyed the patronage of the
countess; but he was probably seeking it.

The early influence of Daniel on Drayton is very extensive.
Though the latter must have read the French sonneteers, his
poems offer no instances of direct translation. On the other hand,
he shows an awareness of Daniel whom he imitates in his sonnets,
and whose *Rosamond* he names in the opening verses of his *Matilda* (1594). It is significant that in *Ideas Mirrour* his first and last
poems quite closely resemble Daniel's sonnets thirty-nine and
two. It is as if, at the beginning and end of the sequence, Drayton
felt strongly the presence of Daniel. Thus *Delia* thirty-nine begins: "Reade in my face, a volume of despayres,/The wayling Ili-
ades of my tragicke wo." The opening lines of Drayton's first
"Amour" are similar: "Reade here (sweet Mayd) the story of my
wo,/The drery abstracts of my endles cares." Indeed, the whole of
this sonnet is very close in theme, and in recurrence of phrasing
and rhyme, to the Daniel sonnet.

Daniel's second sonnet begins "Goe wailing verse, the infants
of my love,/Minerva-like;" Drayton's sonnet fifty-one opens with
"Goe you my lynes, Embassadors of love," and then proceeds
to an allegorical development of the theme of "Minerva in the

sunne." In the obscure allusions that follow, Minerva may be the Countess of Pembroke; Meridianis, Daniel; the maze, the poem *Rosamond;* and "Marygold," the *Delia* sonnets. Though Drayton, with an echo of Sidney in his dedicatory sonnet, says that he is "no Pickpurse of another's wit," we know that he must not be taken too literally; indeed, we have the examples of his borrowings from Daniel cited above, as well as others in the sequence, namely numbers one, twenty-three, and thirty-eight in Daniel compared respectively with ten, fourteen, and thirty-four in Drayton, to mention only a few.[5] Occasionally, Drayton has caught the quiet of Daniel in these sonnets, but he has omitted the melancholy. The echoes are distinct, but he was a poet too in his own right; and, if here he is not so sweet and smooth as Daniel, he was later to attain another style beyond Daniel's reach. A significant point too is that Daniel's habitual use of the "Shakespearian" form was followed by Drayton, and the example might have been encouraging in turn to Shakespeare.

Though of much greater general interest, the influence of Daniel on Shakespeare's sonnets is less easily demonstrable than it is on Drayton's. First of all, we don't know when Shakespeare's sonnets were first written and circulated before being published in 1609. They are mentioned by Thomas Meres in *Palladis Tamia* (1598), and no doubt many of them had been circulated earlier. Topical references, as in "the mortal moon" sonnet, are inconclusive. Daniel's sonnets, on the other hand, first appeared in print in 1591, and during the whole decade his work was much in the public eye, as numerous tributes to him attest. On the basis of known fact, priority seems to be clearly on his side. But that does not mean influence; indeed, a quite recent study goes back to earlier minority arguments that a detailed examination of structure, imagery, meter, and other qualities in the two poets fails to show any Daniel influence on Shakespeare; rather, it says, the influence appears to be the other way round.[6]

This conclusion runs counter to the majority judgment.[7] According to this view, the more important similarities in Shakespeare's sequence to Daniel's are found in the first nineteen sonnets, which correspond to the first eight in the 1592 edition of *Delia,* in which the mistress is urged to surrender to love while she is still young (though Daniel has little to say of marriage and increase) and is promised immortality. Sonnets nine and ten in Shakespeare show some stylistic resemblances to *Delia,* and there are verbal parallels between twenty-four and sixty-four in Shakespeare, and thirteen and thirty-seven in Daniel, respectively.[8] One scholar, after providing a list of parallels, concludes that the greatest resemblance is in tone and style, in the beauty of isolated lines, in the same graceful and easy movement, and in similarity of rhyme scheme.[9]

One of the more striking parallels is that between Daniel's fourth and Shakespeare's second sonnet. Here we find in Daniel, "and all the world may view/Best in my face, how cares hath til'd deepe furrowes"; and in Shakespeare, "When fortie winters shall besiege thy brow/And dig deep trenches in thy beauty's field." To this might be added Shakespeare's sixtieth: "Time doth transfix the florish set on youth,/And delves the parallels in beauties brow." These resemblances may not be conclusive, but it would be strange indeed if Shakespeare, who was quick to imitate anything worthy at hand and to turn it to his own use, should have passed up the first clearly articulated sonnet sequence to be published in the 1590's—in the "Shakespearian form," with many of the sonnets linked too. In fact, Shakespeare had in Daniel an excellent model from which to work: a slow meditative verse, with a touch of melancholy; a command of form; and such fine effects in assonance as "Whose feete doe treade greene pathes of youth and love."

The whole matter of influence has been well put by J. Q. Adams: "Thus in choosing his model Shakespeare, as was usual with him, reflected contemporary taste. From Daniel's sonnets he took his form, acquired much of his sugared style, borrowed not a little imagery and thought, echoed occasional phrases, and learned the trick of nicely linking his poems together. . . . Thus his cycle came to differ from its model in a way that has led scholars to underestimate his really important indebtedness to the *Delia* sequence." [10]

III The Complaint of Rosamond *and Its Origins*

On the title page of *Delia and the Complaint of Rosamond* in 1592 and of many of Daniel's subsequently published works appeared this motto from Propertius: *Aetas prima canat Veneres, postrema tumultus* (youth sings of love, and age of war). Such a modest claim we might expect of Daniel, who, in publishing the sonnet and love complaint, was acting in accordance with good established Classical and contemporary practice. Virgil had begun with the pastoral and had moved on to the epic; Spenser was doing likewise; and Sidney's progression from *Astrophel and Stella* to the *Arcadia* might also be seen as another example of the poet's progress. Daniel's persistent use of the motto is clear indication that he could not, or would not, as a serious, dedicated poet evade his mission; sooner or later he would have to venture on the epic.

He was not alone in realizing the high destiny thrust upon him. The Countess of Pembroke, as we have seen from Daniel's 1594 dedication to *Cleopatra*, had by that time urged him on "to sing of State, and tragicke notes to frame." Spenser in *Colin Clouts Come Home Again* (written in 1591, though published later) reviewed the current state of English poetry and singled out Daniel by name. He must have greatly admired Daniel's sonnets, which he had probably seen in manuscript; but he too expected higher achievement from him:

> And there is a new shepheard late up sprong,
> The which doth all afore him far surpasse:
> Appearing well in that well tuned song,
> Which late he sung unto a scornefull lasse.
> Yet doth his trembling Muse but lowly flie,
> As daring not too rashly mount on hight,
> And doth her tender plumes as yet but trie,
> In loves soft laies and looser thoughts delight.
> Then rouze thy feathers quickly, Daniel,
> And to what course thou please thy selfe advance:
> But most me seemes, thy accent will excell
> In Tragick plaints and passionate mischance.

From these lines it is clear that Spenser had read only Daniel's sonnets. Very likely *The Complaint of Rosamond* had not yet been written, and Daniel was soon encouraged to write it as an example of the tragic plaint and passionate mischance for which Spenser thought him so well fitted.

The Complaint of Rosamond proved to be even more influential than the Delia sonnets. Although less commonly known today than formerly, despite frequent inclusion in anthologies, it still has a strong interest for its historical and artistic origins and for the precise way by which it fused a variety of literary conventions and gave shape and temper to the work of other poets immediately following Daniel, who brings tragic conflict for the first time into union with Renaissance erotic narrative and medieval "complaint."

The chief source for this popular poem was the *Mirror for Magistrates,* and especially two poems in its second edition of 1563: Sackville's "Induction" and Churchyard's "Shore's Wife." The earlier *Mirror* differed in its treatment of tragedy from its medieval models, Boccaccio and Lydgate, by presenting the ghosts of men of high estate that actually tell their own stories and thus enhance the dramatic effectiveness. Sackville's "Induction" introduced a new and alien element into the *Mirror*—the vision of the descent into hell derived from Virgil and Dante. Churchyard's somewhat sentimental poem provided new subject matter for later exploitation—a king's seduction of a beautiful young woman, her remorse and death, and the return of her ghost to claim our sympathy. Such was the method and the general type of narrative that Daniel had before him in composing *Rosamond.* For his plot he drew upon the many chroniclers who had told the story of Henry the Second's seduction of Rosamond Clifford—a mixture of history and legend. The fact that, like most of the narratives contained in the *Mirror,* Daniel's poem dealt with English history must have contributed to its vogue at a time when the popular appetite for history and for moral example was strong.

The first sixty-three lines of *Rosamond* constitute the frame in which the story is set. In this section the remorseful ghost of Rosamond appears from the infernal deeps, where she is denied Elysian rest until her soul is transported by lovers' sighs on earth. Like Shore's wife, she laments that no muse has labored in her behalf; then she asks the aid of the poet, who she hopes may induce Delia to read her story and offer up sighs helpful to both her and the disdained poet. Hopeful that he may forget his own grief, the pitying poet asks for her story, which Rosamond then implores him to write as an example to others. With this moralizing touch, reminiscent of the *Mirror,* the story proper begins. Rosamond tells of her birth and education and of her happy youth spent in the country. Her friends had sought to raise her to higher place by bringing her to court; there her beauty soon attracted the attention of all.

King Henry, she continues, was vanquished at a glance. Chaste in thought, she tried to repel the advances of this aged lover, who now used a "seeming matron" but "sinful monster" to wear down Rosamond's resistance by promises of tempting rewards. Her will was in the balance, but at last she took the course of sin. Quickly she was lured from court to a solitary grange, whither the king sent a marvelous casket on the lid of which was engraved Neptune's seduction of Amymone and the affliction of Io—a prefiguration of her own woe. With night came Rosamond's shame and remorse.

To keep his rich prey the king built a stately palace with intricate passages, where Rosamond became "the Minotaure of shame." The king alone could come to her, and he only when guided by a thread. His jealous queen at last entered the labyrinth, surprised Rosamond, and in a rage forced her to take poison. The dying Rosamond, so her ghost now tells the poet, then delivered the conventional "complaint," moralizing over her fall and hoping to be a "mirrour" to other fair women. The ghost of Rosamond next describes her burial, philosophizes over how ephemeral is fame when expressed in stone, and hopes for immortality through the poet's "favourable lynes." The last forty lines thus return to the frame, as Rosamond announces that she must proceed to Styx and offers thanks in advance to Delia. She vanishes, leaving the poet "to prosecute the tenor of his woes."

Daniel made significant contributions to the story as he adapted it from his sources. In addition to assigning the poisoning to the queen, he introduced the old matron with her persuasive theme of *carpe diem*, the mythological casket decorations prefiguring Rosamond's destiny, and the solitary grange.[11] By substituting the wicked matron for the messenger in earlier versions of the story, Daniel shifted some of the moral responsibility from Rosamond and extended the popular debate on chastity.[12] The casket contributes to the subtlety of the tragedy; for, while Rosamond is responsible, dimly revealed fate also plays a part. As one writer has stated, "Fate worked her fall, yet made the fault still hers."[13]

Although *Rosamond* shows some resemblances to the tragedy

of "Eleanor, Duchess of Gloucester," in the 1578 *Mirror*—particularly in the willfull pride and beauty of the central women characters—it owes more to Churchyard's tale of Edward IV's mistress. Daniel intimates this influence in a reference to "Shore's Wife" at the outset of his poem. There are obvious parallels between the two works: a woman rises from her grave in search of an audience and is burdened with a sense of shame over past sins committed with a king whom she had once proudly dominated. Daniel's poem is clearly the superior: the story is more closely joined with its frame; Rosamond is herself more dignified and restrained as a character; and the use of the casket as both decoration and theme has no counterpart in "Shore's Wife."

Sackville's "Induction" perhaps made a more subtle contribution to Daniel's poem, for it provided a larger framework for rationalizing the appearance of the ghost. But *Rosamond* differs from its predecessors in minimizing the abhorred wickedness of the complainant and in presenting a partial vindication of her through the enlistment of our sympathy. For this purpose the poet must himself get within the framework and, in a sense, join the action of the poem. For this participation Daniel had the example of the "Induction" in which illusion is achieved not by asking the reader to imagine or to suppose or to accept the relation as from a dream, but by placing the poet himself as narrator within the framework. Daniel rounds out his poem by a return to the frame, which Sackville too might have done had he written the new and revised *Mirror* which he is thought to have planned. What both poets do is to dispense with the old *Mirror* concession to literalness and probability in such phrases as "Thinke that you see him standing" or "Imagine that you see him holding his heart in his hand," along with the frequent assurances that what we have heard is either all a dream or a tale coming from an imaginary ghost. They drop these pretenses and put the reader imaginatively in the same world with the characters. Daniel carries further than Sackville this illusion of reality by a convention that offers no apologies, and the poems that come after *Rosamond* follow more or less his example.[14]

Despite resemblances in mood, tone, and inspiration between these two poems, there are marked differences too. Daniel's infernal background is vague and shadowy, like Rosamond herself; but

Sackville's poem is filled with realistic detail reminiscent of Chaucer.

Such are the principal sources from which *Rosamond* grew and the various ways in which, by differing from those sources, it became popular and widely imitated throughout the 1590's. The poem is not without faults: the moralizing is at times heavy; the narrative could do with more action; and the conflict in Rosamond, although the poet handles it with great subtlety, is at last determined by a fear of the world's false opinion if she rejects the king. But the poem, a *tour de force* in its own day, inaugurated the fashion of connecting a narrative poem with a sonnet sequence and even incorporating sonneteering devices within the poem itself. *Rosamond* was actually a fusion of the older *Mirror* and vision types with the newer amatory vein of the sonnet. Furthermore, Daniel's presentation of conflict in the soul of Rosamond was important in the developing conceptions of Elizabethan tragedy. Finally, the poem was an extremely well-told story that offered an improved narrative technique. The artistic success of *Rosamond* is shown by the extensive influence it exerted over the many "complaints" and other forms of narrative poetry in the decade or so after 1592.

IV *The Vogue and Influence of* Rosamond

Among the first to reflect this influence was Anthony Chute in *Beawtie Dishonoured* (1593), a reworking in wretched verse of Churchyard's old tale of Shore's wife; but it has also many traces of *Rosamond* in characterization and in phrasing. In the same year Churchyard himself was prompted by Daniel's success to issue a revision of his earlier poem but without conspicuous borrowings from the new model. Also in 1593 appeared Thomas Lodge's rambling poem *Elstred,* a double "complaint" of mother and daughter that is excessive in its emotion. It contains numerous parallels with *Rosamond,* including the use of similar framework, the employment of the familiar shrouding sheet, and the resorting to identical metaphors and rhetorical devices. Drayton wrote several narrative poems more or less traceable to *Rosamond;* of these, his *Peirs Gaveston* (1594) borrows most heavily. Although this highly sensuous, erotic poem derives partly from other contemporary sources, such as Lodge's *Scillaes Metamorphosis* and Shakespeare's *Venus and Adonis,* we see Daniel's presence most clearly in Drayton's treatment of the honorable burial, the neglected tomb, the gratitude of the ghost for the poet's services, the request for the intercession of the poet's mistress, the ghost's wandering from the Stygian lake, Charon's barge, the labyrinth, and in many close parallels of phrasing and verse.[15] Only slightly less influenced was Drayton's *Matilda* (1594), and to a lesser extent we find the mark of *Rosamond* on still other poems of his: in *The Tragicall Legend of Robert, Duke of Normandy; i*n his longer poem of civil war, *Mortimeriados,* both in 1596; and in two of his Heroical Epistles (1597) dealing with the story of King Henry II and Rosamond. Thomas Middleton's *Ghost of Lucrece* (1600) and Patrick Hannay's *Sheretine and Mariana* (1622) are among the many other poems of the time which derive at least in part from *Rosamond.*

One of the greater erotic poems of the decade to be influenced by *Rosamond* was Shakespeare's *Rape of Lucrece* (1594), written likewise in rime royal stanza. It has long been recognized that *Lucrece* is considerably indebted in general treatment, imagery, and diction to *Rosamond.* Although the poems differ in point of view, both are concerned with the themes of chastity and of remorse for sin. Shakespeare's elaborate mural painting comes at a different psychological moment in his narrative than Daniel's casket in *Rosamond,* but it is likely that this piece of embroidery was suggested by Daniel's poem. Lucrece's long lament bears a general resemblance to Rosamond's, but Shakespeare's poem as a whole is not framed as a "complaint." A few of the more striking parallel images are those of time's cancellation of beauty, the Cross, the face as a book, the silent rhetoric of the eye, might as mother of sleep and fear, and the rose amid the thorns—all of which have been previously noted.[16] Lucrece too must "sell her joy" (385) much as Rosamond (310) must sell herself to lust. Finally, Shakespeare may have obtained the hint for one of his most sustained figures from Daniel's poem. Describing the eventful night when the king came to her, Rosamond (436) tells of the lover for whom she had no love, and adds that she "felt the hand of lust most undesired." This striking figure, sinister in its impersonality, reminds us of the scene in Lucrece's chamber in which the metaphor of the hand besieging the fortress of her chastity sets the stage for her ruin.[17]

Of the many parallels that have been noticed between *Rosamond* and Shakespeare's *Romeo and Juliet*, the most striking is that between King Henry's lament over his dead mistress and Romeo's speech at the sight of the supposedly dead Juliet in the tomb. Rosamond's succumbing to death is thus described: "When naught respecting death, the last of paines,/Plac't his pale collours, th'ensigne of his might,/Upon hys new-got spoyle before his right . . ." (605–7). And the king sees Death as enacting the role of Love, dallying with her as the king himself plants upon her pitiful mouth "this sorrowing farewell of a dying kisse" (669). Shakespeare's Romeo in turn addresses his beloved:

> O my love! my wife!
> Death, that hath suck'd the honey of thy breath,
> Hath had no power yet upon thy beauty;
> Thou art not conquer'd; beauty's ensign yet
> Is crimson in thy lips and in thy cheeks,
> And death's pale flag is not advanced there.   (V.iii.91–96)

Then Romeo envisions "the lean abhorred monster" lying with Juliet as a paramour, just as her distraught father (IV. v. 35–40) had elaborated on this grim metaphor when he first heard of her supposed death.

The extensive popularity of *Rosamond* in its first decade is not hard to understand. It has some rich lines, and the metaphors are often fresh and tender: "Thou must not thinke thy flowre can always flourish"; "When my reviving eye had learnt the truth,/That it had powre to make the winter greene"; "So did my speech when rubies did unfold it." Daniel renders Latin Seneca into an exquisitely sententious English line: "For light cares speake, when mightie griefes are dombe." Admirable too is the poet's scrupulous honesty about the mortality of all things, including his own work; thus Rosamond addresses him toward the close of the poem: "Few in this age had knowne my beauties praise./But thus renewd, my fame redeemes some time,/Till other ages shall neglect thy rime." And then she looks ahead to the time when all music will be silent and the muses dumb, when all that will be remembered is that these arts once flourished in England: "And Thames had Swannes as well as ever Po."

In this poem Daniel managed to do a number of things extremely well, and naturally his work was imitated. It attains a proper fusion of history, myth, and emotional expression; and it subordinates these to the larger design embodied in the haunting beauty of its central figure. The *Delia* framework gives to the narrative of *Rosamond* an additional charge of personal feeling which never becomes obtrusive. By keeping within the confines of his single narrative, and by his judicious use of the details available from his sources, Daniel achieves a unity that is lacking in some of the poems modeled after *Rosamond*. Not heavily freighted with incident, the poem has an air of repose and charm.

Opinion about *Rosamond*'s merits has varied. Praised highly in its own day by Marston, Drayton, and many others, it was cited to the Puritan detractors of poetry by Thomas Nashe in his usual uncompromising vein: "And you shall finde there goes more exquisite paines and puritie of witte, to the writing of one such rare poem as *Rosamond* than to a hundred of your dunsticall sermons." [18] Curiously enough, the English Romantics—Southey, Hazlitt, Lamb, Wordsworth, and Coleridge, who were so strongly attracted to the moral elevation of Daniel's thoughts and to the dignity and calm of certain of his later works, were unimpressed by *Rosamond*. To Wordsworth, the poem was "prolix and dull throughout," even "disgusting," since it contained "few touches of passion"; and he is at a loss "to find out how it ever could be popular." [19] In our time most critics and readers accord it a place among the best poems of the period.

But no doubt exists about the immediate popularity and influence of *Rosamond*. With *Delia*, it established Daniel among the select poets of the decade. Youth had sung softly of love, but his poem of war was not far off. Before that time, his Muse was to mount a step higher in "tragick plaints and passionate mischance."

CHAPTER 3

Senecan Closet Drama (1593-1607)

WHEN Spenser, recognizing Daniel's superior gifts as a poet, urged him shortly after 1590 to higher flights by attempting "tragic plaints" and the theme of "passionate mischance," Daniel was perhaps looking beyond *Rosamond* to the drama about Cleopatra. About the same time (1590) the Countess of Pembroke's translation of the French tragedy *Antonie* evidently encouraged the poet, who gives us the impression at several stages of his career of being pushed, almost against his will, into new endeavor. Such an impression fits well with the modesty and diffidence we associate with Daniel's name—and these characteristics he may have cultivated with both humor and profit.

The opening lines of his dedication of *Cleopatra* to the countess in 1594 lay the finished work assigned him before us: "Loe heere the worke the which she did impose,/Who onely doth predominate my Muse." Further on he tells her that he might have gone on singing the praises of Delia indefinitely, except that, "Madam, had not thy well grac'd *Anthony*,/(Who all alone having remained long,)/Requir'd his *Cleopatras* company." And then later in the dedication he suggests an additional motive for undertaking the drama:

> Now when so many pennes (like Speares) are charg'd,
> To chace away this tyrant of the North:
> *Gross barbarism*, whose powre growne far inlarg'd,
> Was lately by thy valiant Brothers worth,
> First found, encountred, and provoked forth:
>
> . . . .
>
> And now must I with that poore strength I have,
> Resist so foule a foe in what I may.

I *The Senecan Background*

The implications are clear. The countess had taken the lead in introducing to her circle the first English version of a French Senecan drama, and in so doing she was acting in harmony with her dead brother's censure in his *Defence of Poesie* of the crude liberties taken with the Classical unities on the English popular stage. Whatever rich contribution Sir Philip Sidney and his illustrious sister made to the growth of English poetry and to English literature generally, they were mistaken in their appraisal of the popular stage. For a little more than a decade the countess encouraged others in her circle, including Daniel, Fulke Greville, Samuel Brandon, and William Alexander to follow her example in *Antonie* by writing Senecan closet drama.

Seneca, who had written Latin tragedies on Greek themes, had managed to make rigid and lifeless the organic vitality of Greek tragedy. This effect is particularly notable in his choruses, which seem divorced from the action and, in their isolation, become a medium for moralizing. His messenger, instead of being a part of the dramatic action, becomes more and more an epic narrator. In short, dramatic action gave way more and more to lengthy rhetorical declamation, larded with phrase-making and proverb-mongering. All of the English writers just mentioned exhibit these qualities: Daniel's writings, including the nondramatic poems, display a propensity for *sententia* and proverb, and Fulke Greville has so much of it as to become tedious and dull. In Senecan tragedy horror also replaces the terror of Greek tragedy, and personal revenge supersedes the retribution of the gods.

The influence of Seneca remained strong throughout the Middle Ages and the Renaissance, and in the sixteenth century he was much better known and more easily assimilated into popular drama than the more recently rediscovered Greek tragedy. Hence, Seneca remained the principal force, though he also underwent many modifications in shaping the Renaissance drama of Italy, then of France. From Italy the "purer," more rigid and formal, Senecan drama passed into France; there it withdrew farther and farther from the public view and became the closet drama which the Countess of Pembroke and the little group about her were now to cultivate. In Italy another Senecan tradition had also been

established by the absorption of popular elements into its structure, whereby fuller rein was given to the Senecan propensity for
sexual themes and atrocious deeds. This Italian Senecanism does
not strictly adhere to the Classical unities, and it makes common
use of the double plot and of the happy ending. Freighted with
ghosts, furies, dreams, and oracles, this Senecan drama reached
the English popular stage and exerted a powerful influence upon
Thomas Kyd, Christopher Marlowe, Shakespeare, Cyril Tourneur,
and many others. Thus from Italy came two Senecan strains: the
French, with its stiff undramatic and academic formalism that
was doomed to fail from the start; and the English, with its more
popularly based sensationalism and romanticism.

In France, Jodelle's *Cleopatre* (1552) had very little success,
even at court; and, as drama of this kind lost more and more in
popular appeal, it grew more narrow and restricted, more solemn
and decorous. Sexuality and violence are generally avoided in the
plays of Robert Garnier (1545–1601), the chief writer of French
Senecan drama, whom Daniel might very well have met on his
first visit to France, or at some later time. These plays, both the
French and the English imitations of them, seem never to have
been intended for acting but for reading.[1]

The first English attempt to naturalize French Senecan drama,
the Countess of Pembroke's translation of Garnier's *Antonie*, illustrates the tradition to which the countess was showing the way in
her Wilton circle. Though published in 1592, her translation was
completed two years earlier, as her note at the end shows: "At
Ramsburie. 26 November. 1590." Through Act III her play has
little action: Antony laments his weakness in surrendering all his
power and dignity to sensuality though he is still bound to Cleopatra. She, in turn, is ashamed of her cowardly conduct at Actium
and wants to do something generous for the defeated Antony,
who at the same time suspects that she will desert him for Caesar.
First, she wants to convince him of her loyalty and has the message of her death sent to him. Both engage in self-debate and long
speeches, which constitute about all the action until Act IV, when
things begin to stir. In it Dircetus returns to Caesar, who has just
assured Agrippa that he wants Antony dead, with the news that
Antony, falsely informed of Cleopatra's death, had then fatally
wounded himself before being pulled up into Cleopatra's monu-

[44]

ment to die. Caesar wants to get to the Queen before she does violence to herself or cheats him of her hoarded treasure. Nearly all of this fourth act is "staged" in the presence of Caesar in the form of narration by a messenger. In the fifth act, Cleopatra is on stage; disconsolate, she bids goodbye to her children, and then finally expires.

The foregoing summary indicates the kind of play that attracted the interest of the Wilton circle. A typical Senecan device is shown in the formal balancing of an ironic situation: love for the seemingly faithless Cleopatra and humiliation at his own defeat by Octavius led to Antony's suicide; loyal and genuine love of Antony and fear of her humiliation at the hands of a victorious Octavius bring about Cleopatra's suicide. The two principal characters never meet on stage in the play; their encounters are only reported. There is little or no dramatic unity, and the successive acts do not develop from one another. The choruses, however, have a lyrical quality that is the achievement of both Garnier and his able translator. The Egyptian chorus at the end of Act II voices for the first time in the play an idea in rudimentary form that becomes a dominant note in Daniel, when it concludes that Rome too shall in course of time suffer:

> All things fixed ends do staie,
> Ends to first beginnings fall.
> And that nought, how strong or strange,
> Chaungles doth endure alwaie,
> But endureth fatall change.[2]

II Daniel's Cleopatra

Daniel's *Cleopatra* is a much superior play; in fact, it is the best of the English Senecan group. Although he follows his French sources in Jodelle and Garnier, the result, considerably more than a translation, bears some effective dramatic and choral features, as well as many passages of moving beauty.

By beginning with Antony already dead and by focusing on Cleopatra, Daniel's play achieves a unity lacking in the earlier tragedy. His *Cleopatra* has less reported action than *Antonie*, or it may seem so because the reports are more direct and less hazy from being so many removes from the action. Cleopatra's motives for action also seem stronger and more convincing, as when she is deterred from immediately taking her life because she seeks to "purchase grace/for my distressed seede after my death" and to secure assurance of their safety from Caesar. She is not a mere mouthpiece for some abstractly conceived role; she is a warm and sensuous woman whose distress stirs our compassion. Not quite a fully tragic figure, she is decidedly pathetic. Something of Rosamond lingers on in this woman in the proud awareness of her once more enchanting qualities, in her standing at a distance in time and in her assessing her life maturely and philosophically. The tone is well established in these lines:

> For whilst my glory in her greatnesse stood,
> And that I saw my state, and knew my beauty;
> Saw how the world admir'd me, how they woo'd,
> I then thought all men must love me of duety,
> And I love none: for my lascivious Court,
> Fertile in ever fresh and new-choyse pleasure,
> Affoorded me so bountifull disport,
> That I to stay on Love had never leisure:
> My vagabond desires no limites found,
> For lust is endlesse, pleasure hath no bound.   (155–64)

This tragedy possesses a surprising amount of variety and stage action for a play of its kind. In the first act Cleopatra reviews her past and resolves upon eventual death, and then the chorus moralizes on the retribution that is overtaking her. The second act finds Proculeius reporting to Caesar how he has entered Cleopatra's monument and prevented her suicide—how he has persuaded her to live on in amity with Caesar, though she has bitterly opposed the imperial power that threatens to take away even the liberty of being one's self. By contrast, Caesar at the outset of this act had lamented the fact that, while he was all-powerful, he had yet so little power over Cleopatra. Proculeius has wrung from her, it is true, a promise to "sue for grace" on her condition that she may perform the last rites for the dead Antony; but Caesar is suspicious of her. Finally, the chorus speaks of the shifting opinion of men which makes bearable any situation they create and leads them on in restless ambition.

The philosophers Arius and Philostratus introduce Act III with a long discourse on how human suffering can best be borne and how ill-deeds return to plague the inventor. This interesting and eloquently phrased colloquy does bear on Cleopatra's personal tragedy but only in a remote philosophical way that is not dramatically assimilated. It exhibits at once both the attractive and the objectionable qualities of French Senecan drama. In another scene of this act, Caesar, Seleucus, and Dolabella meet with Cleopatra; and Caesar charges that her selfish ambition is the source of all the wrong done. When she insists that only love and loyalty to Antony have guided her, Caesar ambiguously promises her that she will be dealt with as kindly as she can expect, to which she acquiesces and leaves. A new complication occurs as Dolabella is smitten by her charms. Caesar notes it and adds that Cleopatra will be brought to Rome as a prize and trophy. Nemesis (named here for the first time in Daniel's works) is invoked by the chorus as the great arbitress, who brings all transgressors into the full cycle of misery; Egypt, so it says, has its ordained moment of decline and suffering. Here the role of the chorus in sketching in the philosophical background seems appropriate and not dramatically ineffective.

A meeting between the two traitors, Seleucus and Rodon, opens the fourth act. Seleucus, we learn, and by narration only, has tried to sell out to Caesar by betraying Cleopatra and has reaped for his efforts only disgrace. Rodon tells his long story of still another betrayal, of his giving up for execution her son Cesario, and of the boy's long speech before death. Even though the speech is reported, it has race, vigor, and fine narrative speed:

> From *India* (whither sent by mothers care,
> To be reserv'd from *Egypts* common wracke,)
> To *Rhodes* (so long the armes of tyrants are,)
> I am by *Caesars* subtile reach brought backe.   (992–95)

The same scene presents an account of Cleopatra's sentiments as she weighs the opposing arguments for keeping the boy and for sending him away to doubtful safety. In the course of her reported speech she changes her mind half a dozen times, a good example of the Senecan inner debate that is phrased by the poet with convincing dramatic effect. The traitorous servants sneak away as Cleopatra's entrance alone points up a fine contrast in character. And she brings with her a subtly dramatic first hint of Dolabella's visit to her: "What, hath my face yet powre to win a lover?" With some of Rosamond's old vanity, Cleopatra thus exhibits a nice handling of variety and relief. She now knows what Caesar intends and realizes she is past returning Dolabella's love. Paying eloquent tribute to Antony at his tomb, she longs for the time and the means to join him in death and, as the act ends, hints that she has already arranged for that consummation. The usual end-of-act chorus expresses wonder at Egypt's religious decline and develops the idea once again of the ever returning cycle pointing toward Rome, which must carry back from Egypt the seeds of its own ruin.

In Act V, the messenger Titius relates to Dolabella Cleopatra's final renunciation of the latter's proffer of love. All her love is now for the dead Antony, but Dolabella has not given up. His supposing that her message to Caesar merely asks for an audience, instead of for the time she is buying to bring about her own end, is a fine case of the "false dawn." The messenger himself is an actor in these strange events; it is he whom the queen had dispatched to fetch the asps for her death, and he eloquently describes the suicide of Cleopatra and of her maids at the close of the play. The chorus closes on the familiar note of retribution and the eventual overthrow of Rome, as well as of Egypt.

Daniel has invested his story with many passages of great beauty, and nowhere are these more poignant and more dramatically laden than in the messenger's almost conversational description of his return with the deceptive figs to the waiting Cleopatra:

> Well, in I went, when brighter than the Sunne,
> Glittering in all her pompous rich array,
> Great *Cleopatra* sate, as if sh'had wonne
> *Cesar*, and all the world beside, this day:
> Even as she was when on thy cristall streames,
> Clear *Cydnos*, she did shew what earth could shew;
> When *Asia* all amaz'd in wonder, deemes
> *Venus* from heaven was come on earth below.   (1473–80)

Within the undramatic framework of French Senecan tragedy, Daniel imparts a splendor and richness that must have caught the attention of Shakespeare. Through the messenger's story we have a vivid picture of Cleopatra, who, on his return with the concealed serpents "looking among the figs, findes the deceite" (1504). Her words to the serpent a moment later have fine rhetorical balance and word play:

> Therefore come thou, of wonders wonder chiefe,
> That open canst with such an easie key
> The doore of life; come gentle cunning thiefe
> That from our selves so steal'st our selves away.   (1533–36)

We see her at last wavering in her decision to die, with overtones of the earlier loss of her dear Caesarion:

> Looke how a mother at her sonnes departing
> For some farre voyage bent to get him fame,
> Doth entertaine him with an idle parting
> And still doth speake, and still speakes but the same;
> Now bids farewell, and now recalles him backe,
> Tels what was told, and bids againe farewell,
> And yet againe recalles.   (1559–65)

We gaze at her finally with the messenger as her life fades:

> Looke how a new pluckt branch against the Sun,
> Declines his fading leaves in feeble sort;
> So here disjoyned joyntures as undone,
> Let fall her weake dissolved limbes support.
> Yet loe that face the wonder of her life,
> Retaines in death, a grace that graceth death,
> Colour so lively, cheer so lovely rife,
> That none would thinke such beauty could want breath.
> (1635–42)

When in 1607 Daniel made extensive alterations to the play, possibly under the influence of Shakespeare's *Antony and Cleopatra,* this final scene was much shortened, no doubt because the direct presentation of Cleopatra's last moments required less description. Consequently, the gain in dramatic effectiveness was accompanied by some loss in poetic beauty.

The revision of *Cleopatra* in 1607 has significant bearing upon the relationship of Senecan closet drama to the more romantic, popular drama. In the 1594 version of the play Daniel held close to Plutarch's life of Antonius, but he expanded the role of Cleopatra's son Cesario and gave to the queen a mother-love to deepen the pathos. All the principal action, as we have seen—Cleopatra's affectionate leave-taking of her son, the son's going to his execution, and finally the queen's own suicide—is reported, and quite effectively by means of a relaxed verse form—lines of alternating rhyme with occasional blank verse and couplet—admirably suited to dramatic narrative. The principal changes in 1607 were the introduction of new scenes and some rearrangement of old ones, the substitution in some cases of dialogue for long soliloquies and of dramatic action for narrative, and the introduction of several new characters who, instead of having their actions reported, now speak for themselves. Because of this heightening of dramatic effect, it has been generally felt that Daniel was perhaps forced to compromise with the popular drama and that the revised play shows the influence of romantic tragedy.[3] Although there is no evidence that Daniel ever intended *Cleopatra* for stage presentation, enough parallels in action and in phrasing that are not found in Plutarch have been cited to convince us that there is a Daniel-Shakespeare interrelationship in these plays.[4]

A reading of Shakespeare's play and Daniel's revised *Cleopatra* affords two significant conclusions: (1) That portion of new material added to the 1607 version of Daniel's play, material that might have been suggested by either Plutarch or Shakespeare, or both, is narrated rather than cast into dramatic form. (2) With the exception of the final scene (which in its original form already bore high dramatic potentiality), those portions of the early version of Daniel's play that are converted into direct dramatic presentation are almost entirely elements of the story to which Shakespeare gave no attention. The scenes between Caesario and Cleopatra, and later, between Caesario and his guard as he is conducted to his death, owe nothing to Shakespeare and very little to Plutarch. Daniel in these instances worked independently of his usual sources. And in both of his versions he has Cleopatra plan the final catastrophe much more completely than she does in Plutarch and in Shakespeare, and the way in which this episode is handled by the two poets does not suggest influence from Shakespeare.[5]

Daniel and the Countess of Pembroke gave dramatic currency to the Cleopatra story. They were followed by the now virtually unknown Samuel Brandon, who published in 1598 *The Virtuous Octavia.* This play, modeled on Daniel's *Cleopatra,* resembles it in the employment of alternate rhymes and in the dextrous variety of rhyme and meter in the choruses. But the long debates between Octavia and her brother Caesar become wearisome, though the fifth act has an interesting piling up of events. But so much onstage historical time elapses before we hear from the messenger in the final scene of Antony's betrayal by Cleopatra at Actium and of his eventual suicide that we are unconvinced. Brandon lacks the dramatic and narrative skill of Daniel.

Fulke Greville, Lord Brooke, former schoolmate and literary associate of Sidney's and friend and patron of Daniel's, also wrote Senecan closet dramas. One of these has not survived, for, as Greville himself tells us, he sacrificed his *Antonie and Cleopatra* to the fire "not that he conceived it to be a contemptible younger brother to the rest" but that, when he saw its likely application to the Essex conspiracy in 1601, he decided to be more careful "of leaving faire weather behind him." [6] His two surviving tragedies, *Mustapha* and *Alaham,* showing the evils of government under both strong and weak tyrants, are highly abstract and philosophical. He was intensely interested in government and in the state, and ethical and political ideas were more important for him than dramatic form. All three of his plays were probably written before 1600, slightly later than Daniel's. *Mustapha* and *Alaham* have generally the same kind of versification as Daniel's *Cleopatra,* an *ababcc* decasyllabic stanza, though less subtly managed. It seems doubtful that he had any direct influence on Daniel as a playwright at all, although his ethical verse, written around 1600, was very likely an important stimulus to Daniel's thought. Greville's long choruses are really treatises expressing his ideas, and their service is enlisted more for philosophizing than for advancing the plot. Throughout his plays abstract generalizations on power, law, and monarchy are spoken by the characters, often in the form of sententious proverbial comment; and Daniel also makes consider-

[51]

able use of this device in much of his work. Because Greville really had no dramatic gift, his plays, intended as philosophical debates and not for the stage, illustrate the extreme limitations of Senecan closet drama as art.

III   Philotas

Daniel's other Senecan play, *The Tragedy of Philotas,* though not published until 1605, was first conceived, as he states in his Apology to the play, as early as 1596: "Besides above eight yeares since, meeting with my deare friend *D. Lateware,* (whose memory I reverence) in his Lords Chamber, and mine, I told him the purpose I had for *Philotas,* who sayd that himselfe had written the same argument, and caused it to be presented in *St. Johns* College in *Oxford,* where as I after heard, it was worthily and with great applause performed." [7] There is no record that this Apology appeared in print before 1623, but it must have been written no later than 1605. It is clear that, from the time of the meeting with Lateware in the chambers of Lord Mountjoy, who had become Daniel's patron about two years before, Daniel was planning to write another play not long after *Cleopatra.* His Apology then tells how "living in the Country, about foure yeares since, and neere halfe a yeare before the late Tragedy of ours, (whereunto this is now most ignorantly resembled) unfortunately fell out heere in *England,* I began the same, and wrote three Acts thereof, as many to whom I then shewed it can witnesse, purposing to have it presented in Bath . . . as a private recreation for the Christmas."

This statement tells us that three acts were completed in 1600, shortly before the Essex trouble, with no thought at the time that they bore any relation to the Essex plot and that a stage presentation was planned. But we learn later from the Apology that the completion of the play was interrupted by Daniel's obligations to the printer to provide new and revised work. And then —we are not told when—he was "driven by necessity" to write again "and the Stage to bee the mouth of my lines, which before were never heard to speake but in silence." He was reluctant to go to the popular stage, but he consoled himself with the thought that his presenting history in the form of tragedy would have a favorable response from "the better sort of men," now and in time to come

—particularly as he looked at the "idle fictions" and "grosse follies" of the popular stage. So Daniel chose a subject, as he tells us, remote enough in history not to suggest any special bearing on contemporary events. But evidently he miscalculated, for his work was not so construed after he had written acts IV and V in 1604 and probably had had the play performed shortly afterward. For in 1605 he was before the Privy Council for an explanation of the resemblance his play bore to the events leading to the trial and death of Essex in 1601. He denied that there was any connection; but Lord Cranborne, Sir Robert Cecil, who had led the way to the prosecution of Essex, and the Earl of Devonshire, Lord Mountjoy, who for some years had been Daniel's patron and had himself been connected with the Essex plot, apparently resented Daniel's reviving the affair three years after the trial. All this reaction we can infer from the letters that Daniel sent the two noblemen in which he disclaims any connection between the tragedy and current English political history. His later Apology was probably based on what he says in the two letters.[8]

Daniel's account of why he discontinued writing the play around 1600 is plausible. But he might also have recognized that it was too close to contemporaneous events and, with characteristic caution, hesitated. But his reasons for finishing the play in 1604 by adding two acts that are increasingly sympathetic to Philotas (Essex) and treat him as a victim of royal tyranny are less clear. Daniel says that necessity compelled him to finish (and probably stage) the play, though he had already gained favor with the new king and had been made licenser early in 1604 for an acting company, the Children of the Queen's Revels. Since he surely was sensitive enough to know that the Essex affair was still touchy, his insistence that the play bears no resemblance to the Essex plot still leaves his motives open to question. It is significant too that Mountjoy, Sir Thomas Egerton, Lord Howard, the Countess of Bedford, and the Earl of Southampton, who were all intimate with Essex, were held in high esteem by Daniel, who addressed verses of commendation to all of them.[9]

Against this background of controversy and counter-allegation, we may now look at Daniel's Senecan tragedy, uncertain whether it was ever actually staged and aware of the ironies in a closet drama's creating such a public stir. It is a rhymed tragedy, though it contains more blank verse than *Cleopatra;* and Plutarch and Quintus Curtius are the sources. Typically, the drama has relatively little action, has long speeches and choruses of Greeks and Persians at the end of each act, and has the final catastrophe related by a messenger. The verse is somewhat more relaxed and flexible—in fact, more conversational—than that in *Cleopatra.* Philotas, son of Alexander's General Parmenio, is brave and generous; but, at the same time, he is vain and prodigal, as well as contemptuous of Alexander's deification as emperor. Philotas receives a letter from his father warning him to "make himself less than he was," and Alexander has himself already grown suspicious of him, for he has foolishly disclosed too much to his courtesan friend Antigona. In a conversation with the jealous, ambitious Thais, Antigona lets fall Philotas' disparaging remarks about Alexander. She immediately regrets her indiscretion, but too late; Thais has already gone with the report to Alexander's devious and subtle old counselor Craterus. Thus far, there has been no suggestion of a plot led by Philotas.

But the report is only confirming evidence of another charge soon to be lodged against Philotas, to whom word has been brought of a conspiracy against Alexander's life; and he is asked to report it to the emperor. Instead, Philotas does nothing, subsequently testifying that at the time he had thought the information of little moment. When the conspiracy is later surprised and its leader kills himself, Alexander asks Philotas why he has concealed his knowledge of it. The young man eloquently defends his action and is pardoned by the emperor, but only temporarily. For Alexander is next prevailed upon by Craterus and others to seize Philotas and to bring him to trial. During it, Philotas maintains, truthfully it seems, that he has been no party to the conspiracy. Later he is put to torture offstage, as the messenger reveals; and he bears up stoutly while the chorus cheers his fortitude. But at last, as the messenger reports, he broke down and revealed the deeper conspiracy in which both he and his absent father had been involved. Thus his end is anything but heroic. And the long arm of royal tyranny reaches out to strike down his father Parmenio. Touching is the speech of Polidamos, who is sent off by Alexander to murder Parmenio, his old commander:

> But now Parmenio; O, me thinkes I see
> Thee walking in th'artificiall grove
> Of pleasant *Susis,* when I come to thee,
> And thou remembring all our ancient love,
> Hastes to imbrace me, saying, O my friend,
> My deare *Polidamas,* welcome my friend
> Well art thou come, that we may sit and chat
> Of all the old adventures we have run.
> Tis long *Polidamas* since we two met,
> How doth my sovereigne Lord, how doth my son?
> When I vile wretch, whil'st m'answers he attends,
> With this hand give the letter, this hand ends
> His speaking joy, and stabb's him to the heart.
> And thus *Parmenio* thou rewarded art
> For all thy service: thou that didst agree
> For *Alexander* to kill *Attalus,*
> For *Alexander* I must now kill thee.
> Such are the judgments of the heavenly pow'rs,
> We others ruines worke, and others ours.   (1933–51)

The principal action of this tragedy is the trial scene in which the dead conspirator is brought on stage and Philotas is subjected to close questioning by Craterus. At first Alexander is sure that Philotas is innocent, for he doesn't see how a guilty conscience could bear such an open face and exhibit such confidence; but the wily Craterus gradually undermines this impression and fixes more firmly the suspicion in Alexander's mind. We cannot be certain of our own allegiances to these characters. Craterus serves his master with devotion, yet the chorus remarks how great men like Craterus clothe their private hate in the colors of public good. For it is hate—just as much as the facts, which indeed are shadowy—that urges on the court leaders against Philotas. Alexander's course also has not been a wise one, nor can we quite assess his intentions. In the first place, he is taken in by Philotas' appearance; then he is swayed by the court group; and the Greek chorus finally expresses the fear that he, the conqueror of Asia, has in turn been overcome by his own Asiatic trickery and by his pride.

Philotas too is elusive as a character, and we don't know how to assess him. Seemingly innocent, he is guilty; the plot in which he is supposedly involved remains vague; and the author directs our sympathy to him at the end, as his guilt is made to seem something of very limited duration: "Let not my one dayes errour make you tell,/That all my life-time I did never well" (1569–70). And he does not ask so much for life as for the reputation he fears to lose by death. There is ambiguity in all these characters, including the courtesan Antigona. They either do ignoble things or act from ignoble motives, yet they have some nobility of character.

The Essex affair does seem to have affected the structure of Daniel's play, for significant parallels have been found between the recorded court trial of Essex and *Philotas* which are not present in Daniel's sources.[10] Correspondences between Craterus and Cecil, and Philotas and Essex, appear to be more than accidental; and the Essex incident no doubt adds to the confusion and uncertainty of the play, which may also faithfully reflect the confusion, the compromise, and the uncertainty of life as felt by the poet. Nevertheless, the play as a work of art suffers as a consequence.[11]

This tragedy reflects a common concern of all the members of the Wilton group who wrote closet drama—a concern with the limits of government and with the abuse of tyranny. Although the plot is derived from earlier history, the issues are nevertheless contemporary. In the Countess of Pembroke's *Antonie,* in Brandon's *Octavia,* and in Daniel's *Cleopatra* the contemporary overtones may be less prominent than in *Philotas,* but they are present. We know that Greville decided to destroy his tragedy of *Antonie and Cleopatra* because it bore too dangerous a resemblance to the Essex conspiracy. This group of writers, living mostly within the rarefied air of Wilton and Wanstead, the home of Lord Mountjoy, had a distrust of the crowd whom Daniel on other occasions calls "hydra headed." What they wanted was monarchical order, but a responsible and controlled one. We see the abuses of this power in Greville's tragedies and in *Philotas,* which comes closer to contemporary politics than *Cleopatra.* And because it comes so near to the events of Daniel's own day, it has, as might be expected, a resulting confusion of perception—a jostling of the universal and of the particular that impairs a work of art. As a consequence of his involvement with people in high places because of this play, Daniel was hurt; and the incident made an already cautious (and perhaps timid) man still more prudent.

Whatever the history of Daniel's construction and recasting of

Philotas—and we cannot know all the reasons that lie behind it—this play is the least French of its group; and its action is the most theatrical because of an underplot involving Antigona and Thais, a traitor dropping dead, a trial scene, and then a reported torture and confession. There are other signs in the play of relaxation from the more rigid conventions of French Senecan tragedy: a more flexible conversational tone in the dialogue, a chorus that does not appear at the end of Act IV and that resorts to dialogue in Act V, and an evident violation of the unity of time when we learn in Act III that three days have elapsed since the plot against Alexander had first been revealed to Philotas. Daniel's exercise of greater freedom may then have led him, or at least encouraged him, to recast *Cleopatra* in 1607.

It seems pretty clear that Daniel was the most skillful dramatist of his group and that his *Cleopatra* is its most successful effort. French Senecan tragedy was doomed to failure in England, and Daniel apparently saw this fact more clearly than his associates. His "foule foe," the "tyrant of the North, Gross barbarism," which he had sought with his "poore strength" to resist, and indeed did, eventually forced him into compromise and finally into abandonment of closet drama altogether.

CHAPTER 4

Historian in Verse (*1594-1609*)

By 1595 Daniel's reputation was well established. He had shared with Sidney the distinction of inaugurating in print the great outburst of sonneteering in the 1590's; he had given authoritative literary expression to the materials of the chronicles and the *Mirror for Magistrates* in *Rosamond* and had thereby revived the "mirror" poem; he had written the best of the English Senecan dramas. Contemporary allusion frequently placed him alongside Sidney and Spenser. Drayton, near the close of his *Endimion and Phoebe* in 1595, styled Daniel as "the sweet Musaeus of these times" and considered his own invention "meane and base" compared with "Delia's glorious Muse." Similar tributes came from Thomas Nashe, John Marston, Francis Meres, Richard Barnfield, and others.

Perhaps Daniel's reputation in 1595 is best summarized in what William Covel says of him in that curious book *Polimanteia;* offering some brief comment on contemporary writers, the author reserves his most fulsome praise for Spenser and Daniel. England is represented as addressing Oxford University in these words: "And unlesse I erre, (a thing easie in such simplicitie) deluded by dearlie beloved *Delia,* and fortunatelie fortunate *Cleopatra;* Oxford thou maist extoll thy courte-deare-verse happie *Daniell,* whose sweete refined muse, in contracted shape, were sufficient amongst men, to gaine pardon of the sinne to *Rosamond,* pittie to distressed *Cleopatra,* and everlasting praise to her loving *Delia.*" [1]

I *English Historical Epic and the New Patron Mountjoy*

The time was now ripe for a maturing artist, since English poetic form was rapidly becoming a more graceful vehicle for conveying the ever-popular matter of history and its moral lesson. Daniel was only a little more than a hundred years away from the end of the Wars of the Roses and the inauguration of the new Tudor era by Henry VII. The memory of those times coming down through the English chronicles was a still vivid one; and, though the bloodshed and suffering and civil strife were seen as a moral blot, these afflictions could be understood as part of a vast design by which the glorious peace and empire of the Tudors, culminating in Queen Elizabeth, was to emerge. In the hands of certain of the chroniclers and of Elizabethan poets, this view of English history was to take shape as the "Tudor myth."

The historical period thus seen extended from the reign of Richard II, through his deposition and death, to the usurpation of Henry IV and the subsequent strife between Yorkists and Lancastrians, and then to the defeat of Richard III on Bosworth Field and the consequent union of the rival houses in the person of Henry Tudor. It was the period covered by the *Mirror*, Spenser had treated it briefly in his *Faerie Queene*, Daniel was to give this historical span its fullest treatment in narrative verse, and Shakespeare had begun and was to carry on the story as drama in his two great tetralogies: *Richard II, Henry IV*, 1 and 2, and *Henry V;* and *Henry VI*, 1, 2, and 3, and *Richard III*. Daniel's principal sources were Froissart's *Chronicle* (which also was available in Berners' English translation from the French in 1523–25); the various chronicles of Fabyan (1516); Grafton (1569); Holinshed (1587); Polydore Vergil's *History of England* (1534); and Edward Hall's *Union of the Two Noble and Illustre Famelies of Lancastre & Yorke* (1548). It is difficult to say how Daniel made precise use of these sources since there is so much copying and cross-reference among them. For the narrative, Holinshed appears to be the principal base; for the view of English history, with its strong vein of moralizing, Daniel owed most to Hall, who carried on the Tudor myth inaugurated by Polydore Vergil.[2]

The idea of a verse epic on English history was already on Daniel's mind as early as 1593 when writing *Cleopatra*. For, in the dedicatory lines to the Countess of Pembroke, he says:

> And I heereafter, in another kinde,
> More fitting to the nature of my vaine,
> May (peradventure) better please thy minde,
> And higher notes in sweeter musique straine:

> Seeing that thou so graciously doost daine,
> To countenaunce my song and cherish mee.
> I must so worke posterity may finde
> How much I did contend to honour thee.[3]

In other words, the "higher notes" hint at the epic; and the reference to Mary Pembroke's "countenancing" his song so that posterity may see clearly the poet-patron relationship between them indicates that early in 1593 she was still his chief patron. He was probably still tutor to her son, William Herbert.

But there are strong indications that Daniel, whose allegiance and high regard for the countess continued throughout his career, was already drawing away from the rather exclusive association with her at Wilton. He was finding a new and long-continuing sponsor and friend in Charles Blount, Lord Mountjoy, a studious lover of books and later the heroic general of the English forces in Ireland who retrieved Essex' failure in putting down the rebellion there. The *Civil Wars* was first published in four books in 1595 and subsequently appeared with many revisions and additions in 1599, 1601, and 1609. The first edition bears no dedication and no reference to the Countess of Pembroke, but carefully placed near the beginning of the poem appears a fine tribute to Mountjoy:

> And thou *Charles Montjoy* borne the worldes delight,
> That hast receiv'd into thy quiet shore
> Mee tempest-driven fortune-tossed wight,
> Tir'd with expecting, and could hope no more:
> And cheerest on, my better yeares to write
> A sadder Subject, then I tooke before;
> Receive the worke I consecrate to thee
> Borne of that rest, which thou dost give to me.   (I.5)

These lines clearly show Mountjoy to be the new patron, but their position in the poem reveals a decorous, tasteful avoidance of giving offense to the Countess of Pembroke. The new inspiration toward epic poetry, as well as substantial material aid and encouragement, is attributed to Mountjoy and not to the countess, whose interest did not lie in that direction.

Daniel must have come under the patronage of Mountjoy as early as 1593 or 1594. Evidence for this surmisal is in the two surviving manuscripts of the first three books of the poem, one of them an early draft of the first two books, and the other of the third book; and in the first of these the stanza quoted above appears.[4] These must have been written considerably earlier than the date of October 11, 1594, on which the poem was entered in the Stationers' Register. The point is that the *Civil Wars* was begun at least by the time *Cleopatra* was printed, possibly without the countess' knowledge, or at least without her favor, and that Daniel had been cheered on by Mountjoy, who appears over and over again in the poet's later works as a model of the Elizabethan courtier-hero and who finally reaches epic status in the 1607 *Funeral Poem*. An additional point of considerable importance is that such early composition of the *Civil Wars* establishes a prior date for Daniel over Shakespeare for most of the material dealing with Richard II's failure as king and Henry IV's usurpation and death (corresponding with Shakespeare's plays on Richard II and Henry IV). It disposes, in large part, of the claim that in this area of treatment of the Wars of the Roses Shakespeare influenced Daniel. The evidence points to Daniel, after the chronicle sources, as the important literary influence on Shakespeare.[5]

II Civil Wars: *The Shape of the Poem and Its Aims as History*

The *Civil Wars* is more concerned with the historical processes of cause and effect than with heroic exploit. There is too little of the actual physical details of battle deemed necessary in an epic poem, a circumstance which led Ben Jonson to complain that there was not one battle in the *Civil Wars*. Though Daniel dutifully records the battles, he has no real enthusiasm for war; he is more reluctant than Shakespeare, for instance, to dramatize a battle situation, but he sometimes accomplishes the feat, as in the spirited verses describing Hotspur and Talbot. Daniel wants, above all, to show the processes of history at work rather than their particular manifestation in detailed action. And this movement away from the poet to historian is generally evident in Daniel's successive revisions and additions. He becomes more explicit and less metaphorical, more objective and less emotional. He moves from the image to the abstract statement which is inherent in his work from the start. The speeches of his protagonists are masterful in analysis and in suggesting mixed motives, but the climaxes in action usually come to little or nothing.

The poet's references are not always to the past, for he also makes his epic bear directly on present circumstances. One of his most suggestive revisions occurs at the end of Book II in a long passage (stanzas 121–31) appearing in the editions of 1595 and 1599 (it was eventually dropped, except for twelve lines in the later editions). These stanzas deplore the unlawful ground on which the claim of Bolingbroke (later Henry IV) to the crown was based, and they express the wish that the legality of his demand had been commensurate with his real worth. Had it not been for his flimsy claim, civil discord and its attendant bloodshed would not have followed; and England would have been so secure in the centuries ahead that all the world would have bowed to the power of Elizabeth—and Spain would have never dared to meddle in English affairs. Secure in Europe, England might, as champion of Christendom, have carried war to the infidel Turk, with great Essex as its leader, "The *Mercury* of peace, the *Mars* of warre." Then follows a stirring tribute to Lord Mountjoy, after which Daniel renews his speculations on what might have been but for Bolingbroke's guilt. Perhaps the poet would not have been writing of the civil wars, "framing bloudy accents of these times," but might have undertaken the more glorious task of celebrating high achievements under Elizabeth and of eternizing the deeds of those two worthies Essex and Mountjoy. Some of Daniel's most spirited poetry is in this passage. But the fall of Essex forced the poet to omit in 1601 all the stanzas that dealt with him; and in 1609, after Mountjoy's death, almost all the remainder of this long passage was dropped. Daniel's epic had important commentary on his own time, a circumstance which lays open to question the claim he made in 1605 that the story of Philotas was too far removed in time to have any topical reference to current events.

While his theme derived from English history, Daniel drew for Classical inspiration upon Lucan's poem *Pharsalia*, an unheroic epic based on the Roman civil wars. He later calls his poem "my *Homer-Lucan*" in the *Defence of Ryme*,[6] and it has since been noted as the first true imitation in form of the Classical epic in English.[7] For his verse form Daniel chose the ottava rima stanza, in decasyllables of eight lines rhyming *abababcc*, going back to

Tasso and Ariosto, whose *Orlando Furioso* was translated in similar stanza form by Sir John Harington, Daniel's friend, in 1591. It
is a form that, by its recurring rhymes and concluding rests on the
couplet, is eminently suited to a long, slow-paced narrative that
permits reflection and moralizing.

The *Civil Wars* underwent a series of revisions important to our
understanding of the poem and its author. The first four books
were published in 1595, and a fifth was added in 1599. In 1601
many textual revisions were made, and a sixth book was added.
Extensive changes and additions were made also in 1609, whereby
the original third book was expanded to books III and IV; and the
earlier books IV, V, and VI, became V, VI, and VII; and to all
these Book VIII was added. Even so, Daniel had gone only as far
as the middle of Edward IV's reign, and he had not yet dealt with
Richard III's rise to power and subsequent defeat at the hands of
Henry VII. Thus the poem stops about two-thirds the way to its
projected goal. As early as 1601 Daniel seemed to be tiring of the
task, but in 1609 he resumed the project with a renewed vigor and
with an interest that were not, however, to last.

III   Civil Wars: *The Earlier Books*

Daniel's best writing, his most vivid use of metaphor and most
lively re-creation of history is in his first five books, three of which
were already in manuscript before publication in 1595 and all of
which bring to the reader a direct, dramatic account of events
that is less noticeable in the later books. For in these first books
attention is focused mainly on the two central protagonists, Richard II and Bolingbroke. In Book I the quarrel comes to a head,
and Daniel has already attained the objectivity that he maintains
as a cool observer of factional extremes through the poem, although he is morally on the side of legally constituted royalty.
Characteristically, he slows the stanza for measured, sententious
reflection as he looks at both sides: "That we may truly say, This
spoyld the State,/Youthfull Counsaile, private Gaine, partial
Hate" (I.33).

This same distance is attained when the poet tells of Bolingbroke's going into exile (I.67–73). The multitude feelingly addresses an apostrophe to the ocean in protest against his removal
from England. But our sympathy is quickly balanced by the poet's

reflection on the wisdom of the "graver sort" who work for stability against the emotion, the irresponsibility, and the insurrection of the "malecontented sort." Daniel's pronounced conservatism is again shown in the sententious concluding couplet: "Since wise men ever have preferred farre/Th' unjustest peace, before the justest warre." These are the moderating notes in a book that sounds on the whole the theme that violence done to peace must be paid for over and over again.

Bolingbroke has a partially just cause; but, when he breaks exile and returns to his country, the Genius of England (Daniel's own contribution to the story as a kind of dramatized royal conscience) tries to dissuade him from his purpose, which at this point is properly kept vague and uncertain, as it is in Shakespeare; for we cannot distinguish his motive from what fate necessitates. She warns him that "The babes, unborne, shall (o) be borne to bleed/In this thy quarrel, if thou do proceede" (I.89). And ominous signs of the penalty for moral transgression begin to appear later "in lines of fire and characters of blood" (I.113). The whole latter portion of Book I is concerned with fate and individual responsibility as they bear upon Bolingbroke's course of action. He himself seems to be groping and uncertain, resolute man though he is.

The most moving and dramatic part of Daniel's story is in Book II, which offers many parallels in situation with Shakespeare's *Richard II*. We follow the declining fortunes of Richard and grow more sympathetic toward him, once we have looked past his folly and see him wronged. We are never allowed in the course of the poem to forget that Richard's cause was the right one and that nothing can ever justify the usurpation. (At a later time, in the 1609 revision of his poem, Daniel became somewhat less harsh in his judgment of Henry IV, possibly because of the influence of Shakespeare.) The warm sympathy of the poet is felt as he looks upon those who remained loyal to the deserted Richard:

> Time, spare, and make not sacrilegious theft
> Upon so memorable constancy:
> Let not succeeding Ages bee bereft
> Of such examples of integrity:
> Nor thou magnanimous *Leigh* must not be left
> In darknesse, for thy rare fidelity.   (II.26)

The pathetic Richard momentarily believes that Bolingbroke
will prove a loyal subject if only the wrongs done him are righted.
But Montague shows a remarkable knowledge of men in his
weighty speech of advice to the king:

> What hope have you, that ever *Bullingbrooke*
> Will live a Subject, that hath tri'd his fate?
> Or what good reconcilement can you looke,
> Where he must alwayes feare, and you must hate?
> And never thinke that he this quarrell tooke
> To reobtaine thereby his private state.
> T'was greater hopes, that hereto did him call:
> And he will thrust for all, or else lose all.   (II.35)

The king is soon made prisoner, and the poet admirably conveys
both the rush and speed of his movements, as well as his pitiful
plight, in a stanza with a Miltonic ring in its third and fourth
lines:

> To *Flint*, from thence, unto a restless bed,
> That miserable night, he comes convayed;
> Poorely provided, poorely followed,
> Uncourted, unrespected, unobayd:
> Where, if uncertaine sleepe but hoovered
> Over the drooping cares that heavy weigh'd;
> Millions of figures, fantasie presents
> Unto that sorrow, wakened griefe augments.   (II.52)

Richard is now led captive in a procession through the streets of
London as he follows the triumphant Bolingbroke, who is ironi-
cally mistaken by Richard's queen for her own beloved husband:

> Lo, yonder now at length he comes, sayth shee:
> Looke, my good women, where he is in sight:
> Do you not see him? yonder; that is hee,
> Mounted on that white Courser, all in white,
> There where the thronging troupes of people bee;
> I know him by his seate, he sits s'upright:
> Lo, now he bowes: deare Lord, with what sweet grace!
> How long, have I longd to behold that face!   (II.69)

When she learns of his captivity, she controls her welling grief admirably: "Sorrow keepes full possession in her heart,/Lockes it within, stops up the way of breath,/Shuts senses out of doore from everie part" (II. 80). Next she visits the king in prison, and the painful moment of silence, as they gaze at each other with overcharged hearts, is described:

> Thus both stood silent and confused so,
> Their eyes relating how their hearts did morne:
> Both bigge with sorrow, and both great with wo
> In labour with what was not to be borne:
> This mightie burthen, wherewithall they goe,
> Dies undelivered, perishes unborne;
> Sorrow makes silence her best Orator,
> Where words may make it lesse, not shew it more. (II.92)

This stanza is introduced by a single line summarizing the emotional prelude to this moment, it works its way smoothly through an extended metaphor, and it emerges at the close with the generalization born from the sorrow which paradoxically never comes to birth in the actual words of the sufferers. Following the charges brought against him, Richard surrenders his crown; and Book II ends with an indictment of Bolingbroke for having set in motion a long train of disasters that were to afflict England for the next hundred years.

Originally Book III carried the narrative through the murder of Richard, some of the events in the reign of Henry IV, and finally the latter's death. In 1609 Daniel greatly lengthened the disproportionately short account of Henry's reign by expanding this book into books III and IV, and at the same time he toned down his more severe indictment of Henry in the earlier versions. The early portions of this section treat of Henry's failure to reward his followers to their satisfaction. A plot is initiated by the Abbot of Westminster to kill the usurper and to restore Richard. Daniel is at his best here in describing the tortuous workings of thought and motive. The cautious, guarded suggestion put out by the abbot is shown by its effects on the listeners, and the poet characteristically generalizes upon the scene:

> This open-close, apparent-darke discourse
> Drew-on much speech: and everie man replies:
> And every man addes heate: and words inforce
> And urge out wordes. For, when one man espies
> Anothers minde like his, then ill breedes worse;
> And out breaks all in th'end what closest lies.
> For, when men well have fed, th'blood being warme,
> Then are they most improvident of harme.   (III.29)

To the now impetuous conspirators Blunt urges extreme caution in a weighty, well-reasoned speech, and his moderation is justified; for soon the plot is betrayed by Aumerle and punishment from the king comes swiftly to the conspirators. The king now sees the living Richard, though a prisoner, as a constant threat to his security; he gives, therefore, the sign to Exton to murder him. A little later Richard's dying moments are effectively described through a deft succession of metaphors:

> But now, as this sweet Prince distended lay,
> And him nor Life, nor Death, their owne could call,
> (For, Life, removing, rid not all away;
> And Death, though entring, had not seis'd on all)
> That short-tym'd motion had a little stay
> (The mover ceasing) though it were but small:
> (As th'Organ-sound, a time, survives the stop,
> Before it doth the dying note give up).   (III.80)

Henry, now beset with troubles abroad and at home, is aptly described in a passage (IV.10–12) which appeared for the first time in 1609. These stanzas reveal Daniel's considerable ability as a reflective historian who is always able to see at work the larger processes of history. He can also at times treat events with epic vigor and vividness, as when he apostrophizes the king: "There shall young *Hotspur*, with a fury led,/Ingrapple with thy sonne, as fierce as hee" (IV.34). And the language of Hotspur's address to his followers before the Battle of Shrewsbury suggests Shakespeare's Hotspur on the same occasion and Henry V's spirited address before the Battle of Agincourt:

> This day (saith he) my valiant trusty friendes,
> What-ever it doth give, shal glory give;
> This day, with honor, frees our State, or endes
> Our misery with fame, that still shal live:
> And doo but thinke, how well the same he spends,
> Who spends his blood, his Country to relieve.
> What? have we hands, and shall we servile bee?
> Why were swordes made? but, to preserve men free.   (IV.38)

But Daniel cannot sustain the flight and speed; he soon drops to his wonted plane of eloquent reflection upon the broader issues of history. Both of these passages are found in his earliest versions, including the manuscript, as are indeed most of his more vigorous lines.

The early part of the newly reconstituted Book IV of 1609 is pretty much a dull chronicle of events, which improves only with the account of the fighting at Shrewsbury and of the prince's theft of the crown and the death of King Henry. These dramatic stanzas on the crown-stealing were missing from the earlier manuscript and appeared first in 1595. We can thus see how Daniel built in additional dramatic elements later utilized by Shakespeare in 2 *Henry IV*. In this last scene, Daniel's image describing the bodily feebleness of King Henry just before his death is similar to Shakespeare's treatment of the same situation (IV. iv.117–20); and the similarity strongly suggests that Shakespeare was familiar with Daniel's lines:

> Whose harald sickness, being sent before
> With full commission to denounce his end,
> And paine, and griefe, enforcing more and more,
> Besiegd the hold that could not long defend,
> And so consum'd all that imboldning store
> Of hote gaine-striving bloud that did contend,
> Wearing the wall so thin that now the mind
> Might well looke thorow, and his frailty find.   (III.116)

Daniel's attitude toward the kingship is consistent. He recognizes throughout his poem that Richard's cause is more rightful than the usurper's. Even when Henry's ingratitude toward those, like Hotspur, who helped him to the crown is shown and when the personal and individual merit of Hotspur is made evident, the poet still takes the side of the duly constituted king.

The poem has now arrived at the heroic central figure of the civil wars—Henry V, about whom Shakespeare wrote a play that is epic in spirit. What does Daniel do with this figure? Since his fifth book must cover much historical ground, Henry, though glorified, is dealt with briefly. For the poet must not break the unity of his design, which is the civil wars, and not a *Henriad*. He must, of course, offer some justification for such apparent oversight. Accordingly, the narrative is interrupted by the apparition of Henry V, who chides the poet for his neglect and asks that the great actions of his day be celebrated by someone in Elizabeth's time, since her reign "is better graced with those bright ornaments to us denied." The spirit of the dead king asks that the epic deeds of true history be dealt with, as the poet glances perhaps disdainfully at the more fanciful renaissance epic-romance:

> Why do you seeke for fained *Palladines*
> (Out of the smoke of idle vanitie)
> Who may give glory to the true designes,
> Of *Bourchier, Talbot, Nevile, Willoughby?*
> Why should not you strive to fill up your lines,
> With wonders of your owne, with veritie?
> T'inflame their ofspring with the love of good,
> And glorious true examples of their Blood.
>
> What everlasting matter here is found,
> Whence new immortall *Illiads* might proceed!
> That those, whose happie graces do abound
> In blessed accents, here may have to feed
> Good thoughts, on no imaginarie ground
> Of hungry shadowes, wich no profite breed;
> Whence, musicke-like, instant delight may growe;
> Yet, when men all do knowe, they nothing knowe.   (V.4–5)

The poet is to convey the message to Queen Elizabeth "that she repaire what darknesse hath defac't" and order that the deeds of Henry V's own unsung days be "reedified" by some worthy poet. The spirit of Henry also argues the justice of his request by asking whether the queen would want the deeds of *her* day swallowed up in darkness. Daniel is thus enabled to suggest that there is epic matter in his own day to be sung, that some poets the queen actually fosters for this undertaking, and he hints that he is one of them (V.10). He will remain in this poem a Lucan, singing only of civil war, and not venture on Homer's way.

So Daniel, since his subject is civil war at home and only incidentally conquest abroad, moves on with his design, deals very slightly with the epic possibilities of Henry V's exploits in France, and does nothing with the events of Harfleur and Agincourt. Yet in stanza eleven he wishes that someone else might undertake the task. He is concerned with the moral theme that threads its way through the heroic actions to which he deliberately devotes less space; and, after giving a "character" of the king, he returns to the well-documented treatment of the political plots against Henry.

Professor Tillyard observes that Daniel by this action "confesses that he has been a Lucan rather than a Homer and that he intends to omit a present excellent chance of fulfilling the prime epic function of instructing through the examples of heroic deeds, and this confession should strengthen our opinion that Daniel intended to make good his opinion elsewhere." That intention, I believe, was partially made good, as will be seen in Chapter Six in the discussion of the *Funeral Poem on Devonshire*. Tillyard says that, within the *Civil Wars* itself, Daniel partially makes up for the deficiency by resorting to the rhetorical device of listing all the things about Henry he does not deal with, in the course of which "he does indeed deliver an eloquent Panegyric." [8] But surely the effectiveness of this panegyric is exaggerated, for the reader *is* disappointed that Henry must be passed over so quickly despite the poet's avowed determination not to violate the unity of his subject.

IV Civil Wars: *The Later Books*

The seeds of trouble at home in England are already being sown as the death of Henry V occurs, and in these difficulties the poet sees a kind of avenging justice that has dogged his country from the time of Bolingbroke's usurpation: "Neere three score yeeres are past since *Bullingbrooke*/Did first attaine (God knowes how just) the Crowne" (V.45). Shakespeare has Henry IV say much the same thing in his deathbed talk with his son. Shortly afterward we see the infant king Henry VI, whom Daniel rightly describes as a "good" person, but also as "bad" in the interest of his country. His marriage to the French Margaret only intensifies the civil insurrection at home led by the Duke of York. Daniel's portrait of Margaret, generally less favorable than Shakespeare's, is due to something more than fidelity to his sources; it is a manifestation of his deep-seated English suspicion of things foreign. This attitude is shown again in stanzas 86–88; in them—after relating that Humphrey, Duke of Gloucester, the king's advisor, dies under suspicious circumstances, possibly through poisoning—Daniel's chauvinism breaks out: "Are these the deedes, high forraine wittes invent?/Is this that Wisedome whereof they so boast?" Let them keep to their vile cunning, he says, "And let the *North* (they count of colder blood)/Be held more grosse, so it remaine more good." Daniel will have none of their contagious iniquity, which he asks Neptune to bar from his native shore and "keepe us mere English."

With the queen and her minion Suffolk free for a moment, the latter is charged with mismanagement and sent into exile; but he never gets out of England: he is murdered on the beach at Dover, his head is cut off, and his body is left on the sand. The episode is handled with grim sententiousness by the poet: "Part of his blood hath *Neptune*, part the Sand,/As who had mischiefe wrought by sea and land" (V.101). The queen's fierce grief is next described, and the book ends with the outbreak of Cade's rebellion, which, though secretly countenanced by the Duke of York, is finally put down. Daniel has no sympathy for Cade, who is but another manifestation of the many-headed hydra, the mob.

With Book VI (originally Book V and first published in 1599) comes the long account of Nemesis, one of the key passages in the poem. The Duke of York, having taken his position close to London, plants his artillery outside the city. At this point the poet creates a nostalgic picture of medieval Europe before gunpowder came into use:

> It was the time, when faire *Europa* sate
> With many goodly Diadems addrest;
> And all her parts in florishing estate
> Lay beautiful, in order, at their rest:
> No swelling member, unproportionate

Growne out of forme, sought to disturbe the rest:
The lesse, subsisting by the greaters might;
The greater, by the lesser kept upright.

No noise of tumult ever wak't them all:
Onely, perhaps, some private jarre within,
For titles, or for confines, might befall;
Which, ended soone, made better love begin:
But no eruption did, in generall,
Breake downe their rest, with universall sin:
No publique shock disjoynted this faire frame,
Till *Nemesis* from out the Orient came.   (VI.28–29)

This hushed world is almost like that which Milton prepares for the birth of Christ in his Nativity Ode.

Daniel has here brought English history into the larger context of world history, and he shows Nemesis as a force that ranges through the actions of all men. From the start, the conception of Nemesis as a principle of justice that dogs the wrong-doing of man and allows no one people to remain forever in prosperity was in the *Civil Wars*. Thus "wrong revenging *Nemesis*" appears in 1595 (IV.35) and in the still earlier manuscript of Book III. But Daniel in the sixth book expands the function of Nemesis enormously:

Fierce *Nemesis*, mother of fate and change,
Sword-bearer of th'eternall Providence
(That had so long, with such afflictions strange,
Confounded *Asias* proud magnificence,
And brought foule impious Barbarisme to range
On all the glory of her excellence)
Turnes her sterne looke at last unto the West;
As griev'd to see on earth such happy rest.   (VI.30)

And now she calls upon Pandora to destroy the peace of those pious medieval builders of temples by tricking them with the offer of more knowledge. So Pandora, like Eve tempting Adam, presents the fatal gifts of printing and artillery—gifts that will be used by unworthy men to subvert the old order. Printing is seen as an art

> Whereby, the vulgar may become so wise,
> That (with a self-presumption over-growne)
> They may of deepest mysteries debate,
> Controule their betters, censure actes of state.   (VI.38)

And confusion becomes confounded by the horrible introduction of artillery: "For, by this stratagem, they shall confound/All th' antient forme and discipline of Warre" (VI.40). And then men ransack nature to make their devilish engines of cunning. Perhaps Milton in his description of Mammon's searching for treasure (*Paradise Lost* 1.685–88) had Daniel's account in mind:

> And boldly breaking with rebellious minde
> Into their mothers close-lockt Treasurie,
> They Mineralls combustible do finde,
> Which in stopt concaves placed cunningly
> They fire.   (VI.49)

Pandora is next represented as concurrently engaged in upsetting the balance in Europe by making the larger states absorb the smaller ones and by stirring up factions in England. For this fanciful version of history Daniel has been criticized: first, for the mixing of myth with his ostensibly historical narrative; and, second, for his faulty interpretation of the facts of Europe's real condition at the end of the Middle Ages. In his defense it may be said that he does not call printing a wholly evil thing; it is such only insofar as its uses are perverted. Nor does he elsewhere take a romantic view of the Middle Ages and eulogize its chivalry: "Let others sing of knights and paladins" he has said more than once in his works. What he gains by the Nemesis passage, as Tillyard has said, is "an enlarged picture of history" and with it "an enlarged picture of God's way with nations," which transcends the "Aeschylean scheme of the Wars of the Roses." God's way cannot "allow perpetual prosperity," and the Nemesis that swept away the simple, pious life of the Middle Ages was God's agent.[9]

Near the close of Book VI is the section on Talbot's heroic action at Bordeaux (76–97). This longest, most exciting piece of battle action in the whole poem is worthy to stand beside Shakespeare's similar treatment of the same character in 1 *Henry VI*. We see Talbot facing superior odds, as Daniel successfully con-

veys a swiftly moving succession of images that occupy a point
halfway between tangible objects and abstract ideas:

> For, though he saw prepar'd, against his side,
> Both unlike fortune, and unequall force,
> Borne with the swelling current of their pride
> Downe the maine streame of a most happy course:
> Yet stands he stiffe, undasht, unterrifi'd;
> His minde the same, although his fortune worse:
> Virtue in greatest dangers being best showne;
> And though opprest, yet never over-throwne.   (VI.78)

The undaunted Talbot cheers up his soldiers by admitting that
they are outnumbered by the enemy, but he also says that this
very fact will redound to their glory. We think of Shakespeare's
presentation of Hotspur's comforting his associates with the same
argument before the Battle of Shrewsbury as we listen to Talbot:
"And what if there be come some more then they?/They come to
bring more glory to the day" (VI.80). The next stanza begins with
"Which day," and later it again picks up "This day". Daniel's Hotspur and Talbot and Shakespeare's Henry V all resort to the
phrase, which becomes a kind of epic formula. Talbot continues:
"Never had worthy men, for any fact,/A more faire glorious
Theater, then we" (VI.82); and he concludes, "And if we die, that
we di'd not in vaine." The description of the battle that follows
begins with a fine simile: "For as with equall rage, and equall
might,/Two adverse windes combat, with billowes proud" (VI.92).
And then comes the climax of this epic passage, the great stanza
introduced by the beautifully abstracted metaphor of the wrestling match:

> Whil'st *Talbot* (whose fresh ardor having got
> A mervailous advantage of his yeares)
> Carries his unfelt age, as if forgot,
> Whirling about, where any need appeares:
> His hand, his eye, his wits all present, wrought
> The function of the glorious Part he beares:
> Now urging here, now cheering there, he flyes,
> Unlockes the thickest troups, where most force lyes.   (VI.93)

[74]

Talbot fights bravely on, until at last he falls; and Daniel writes of his end in an epic style which makes the reader yearn for more of the same in the poem:

> Then like a sturdy Oke, that having long,
> Against the warres of fiercest windes, made head,
> When (with some forc't tempestuous rage, more strong)
> His down-borne top comes over-maistered,
> All the neere bordering Trees (hee stood among)
> Crusht with his waightie fall, lie ruined:
> So lay his spoyles, all round about him slaine,
> T'adorne his death, that could not die in vaine.   (VI.95)

In 1601 Daniel made a good many revisions and added a sixth book, later numbered as the seventh, to his poem. Those revisions show him as moving further away from concrete metaphor and hyperbole toward abstraction and correctness. He must have been tiring of his task, for he seems appalled near the end of his new book at the fact that he is only a little more than halfway through his poem, which he is not sure whether he should continue or "leave-off here." This book is the dullest, most prosaic one of all as it threads its way through intrigue and alternate successes and failures to York's death at Wakefield, to King Henry VI's short return to power, and finally to the accession of Edward IV. There are, however, still occasional flashes of fine poetry. Among these are stanzas nine and ten in which one of Daniel's favorite metaphors, the river image, is nicely applied to the drying up of York's hopes and then to their flowing again. And the figure of the young Earl of March as the hunted Libyan lion who rushes out upon his pursuers is especially good (VII.97).

One of the fine things in Book VII is Daniel's account of the growing support given to the Duke of York and of the defection of one of its leaders, Trollope, whose desertion is contrasted with the loyalty of John Blunt. The last four lines of the stanza neatly epitomize the situation; and, of these, the last two, which Daniel retouched in 1609, offer fine contrasts in character by the judicious placing of names, the sensitive use of alliteration and assonance, and an appropriate slowing down in the tempo of the last line, where all is concentrated on Blunt:

Many brave Leaders, that adventured
Their fortunes on the side that he had lay'd:
Whereof as chiefe, *Trollop* and *Blunt* excell'd:
But *Trollop* fayld his friends; *Blunt* faithfull held.   (VII.22)

The *Civil Wars* ends with Book VIII, the one Daniel added in
1609. He brought to this book a great deal more energy and enthusiasm than he had shown in 1601. He seems to have found
himself once more and to be working under some new inspiration.
There is a renewed spring in some of the verse, and we can trace
with interest the varying fortunes of the hapless King Henry. Two
important scenes (Henry's reflections on the mole hill and the woo-
ing of Lady Grey) seem to have come from similar ones in Shakespeare's 3 *Henry VI*, which had been in existence for over fifteen
years by the time Daniel came to the same incidents in his poem.
Daniel's detail in the one scene is reminiscent of Shakespeare; in
the other, both Shakespeare and he greatly elaborate on the
chronicle sources.

When King Edward betrays Warwick, sent to negotiate for his
marriage in France, by marrying the Lady Grey, Warwick goes
into retirement for the time; he flees a world of corruption and
deceit for one of contemplation. But he must return to the active
life, as he tells his confessor who tries to detain him; and he sees
his own course clearly against a background of cosmic order:

I knowe, that I am fixt unto a Sphere
That is ordayn'd to move. It is the place
My fate appoints me; and the region where
I must, what-ever happens, there, imbrace.
Disturbance, travaile, labor, hope and feare,
Are of that Clime, ingendred in that place.
And action best, I see, becomes the Best.
The Starres, that have most glorie, have not rest.   (VIII.104)

This whole colloquy is entirely Daniel's contribution to the story.
Warwick continues:

Besides: it were a Cowards part, to fly
Now from my Holde, that have held out so well;

> It be'ing the Station of my life, where I
> Am set to serve, and stand as Sentinell.   (VIII.105)

The poem ends with Warwick's returning to the world of action.

V   Civil Wars: *Its Place and Rank*

Thus ends Daniel's poem two-thirds the way along to the usual classic twelve books. We are not certain why he failed to conclude it, for there was ample material remaining for the rest of his narrative. Perhaps he had already begun his prose *History* and never returned to the poem. There might have been other reasons too. Though Daniel regularly saw the values of history reflected in the present, he was very cautious about dealing with current topical matter. Perhaps, as his history approached more recent times, he grew more reluctant to go on. Besides, the last great Tudor, Elizabeth, was dead; and there was less incentive under King James to bring the Tudor myth to an end.

As has been said before, Daniel's best work in the *Civil Wars* is found in the first five (actually six) books, mostly written before 1599 but with about half of it in manuscript form possibly as early as 1593. In the early portions the subject is more closely integrated and dramatized than in the later books, which frequently tend to drowse along. But the poem as a whole is informed by a purpose: no people can have unlimited peace and prosperity; for wrongdoing, a nation must pay in suffering; yet out of it comes the shining Tudor achievement. Behind all this suffering is a divine purpose that works through the mind of man. We see the great leaders of the past—"presented as acting in ignorance of their true condition, and instruction is intended to be drawn from the contrast between the passionate partiality of their knowledge and the reasoned completeness of ours." [10] The design unfolds before us as we survey the events from a distance. Hence immediacy, or epic realism, is often sacrificed for a detachment and an irony that provides moral judgment and universal statement. Indeed, Daniel's aim is set forth clearly at the outset of the *Civil Wars* (1.6); the work will be, he says, "Unintermixt with fictions, fantasies./I versifie the troth; not Poetize."

Although, as Drayton said, Daniel was "too much historian in

verse," his poem is something considerably more than mere versification of truth, and he very often does poetize. He has simplicity
and dignity of language; he is economical, often subtle in his de-
ployment of metaphors. Enough of his verse has been quoted
above to show that he is often a moving epic poet—at times, even
an exciting one.

There were other verse treatments of English history in Daniel's
time. William Warner's *Albion's England,* issued in 1586 and subsequently expanded, is a long chronicle, interspersed with leg-
ends, in lumbering fourteeners, with little philosophic design. Michael Drayton, perhaps touched off by the success of Marlowe's
Edward II, published in 1595 his *Mortimeriados,* dealing with the
troubles of Edward II's reign. This three-thousand-line poem in
rime-royal stanza is loose and episodic, but often romantic and
sensuous. When Drayton revised the poem in 1603 as *The Barons Warres,* he appears to have been trying to write a poem like
Daniel's by his employment of the ottava rima stanza; and Drayton's new poem shows a more historical and critical, and less decorative and romantic, treatment of material than his original version. The reflective, analytical passages in Drayton's thoroughly
recast epic exhibit a detachment and intellectual effort that show
Daniel's influence.[11]

In Daniel's time the *Faerie Queene* and *Arcadia* were thought
of as the two great epics of the Elizabethan age, and they have
remained so. Daniel's *Civil Wars,* aiming at historical truth while
trying to remain a poem, lacks the imaginative power of Sidney's
and of Spenser's work. But it is beyond any other epic of its day,
and it must take its place among the first dozen or so poems of its
kind in English.

By 1595 Daniel had undertaken all the kinds of work implied in
his Latin motto from Propertius: *Aetas prima canat veneres postrema tumultus.* In his first age of poetry he had sung of love and
"passionate mischance," and now he had successfully written of
war, of "tumultuous Broyles," the theme of the mature poet. He
was about to enter the second half of his career, taking the lead
among English poets in a variety of new forms.

CHAPTER 5

Poet Philosophical (1598-1603)

D URING the years 1595–1603, Daniel turned to the writing of philosophical and ethical poetry, often in the form of the verse epistle. He was busy revising and repolishing his verse, perhaps encouraged to do so by the criticism of his friend and colleague Hugh Sanford at Wilton, for in Daniel's *Defence of Ryme* (1603), he writes: "Besides, to me this change of number in a Poem of one nature sits not so wel, as to mixe uncertainly, feminine Rymes with masculine, which, ever since I was warned of that deformitie by my kinde friend and contriman Maister *Hugh Samford,* I have always so avoyded it, as there are not above two couplettes in that kind in all my Poem of the Civll warres: and I would willingly if I could, have altered it in all the rest." [1] Examination shows that the poet not only carefully avoided such mixing of rhymes in the *Civil Wars* but also eliminated a great many feminine rhymes already existing in his earlier work.

"Samford," or "Sanford," as he is variously called, must have been highly regarded by Daniel. An elusive figure who passes in and out of view for some fifteen years of the poet's life, Sanford is probably the person commissioned by the Countess of Pembroke to be editor of the 1593 *Arcadia;* in the Preface he spoke very disparagingly of the editor of the 1590 *Arcadia* (probably Florio) and thus provoked Florio in turn to attack him as "H.S." in the Preface to his dictionary in 1598.[2] This "H.S." had called Florio's poet-friend a "rymer," and if, as Florio's biographer assumes, the poet-friend is Daniel, we might suppose that the attack was occasioned by Sanford's jealousy of his successor as tutor. But the whole tone of Daniel's later explanation in the *Defence* indicates friendship and a spirit of helpful criticism on the part of Sanford, also a Somersetshire man. At any rate, at the end of ten years' association Daniel speaks of Sanford with respect.

Whatever his merits in Daniel's eyes, Sanford appears to have been socially graceless. While secretary to the Earl of Pembroke on important negotiating missions for the Herbert family, his tactless behavior to Essex' representatives in a business transaction led to ill-feeling between the Earl of Essex and the Earl of Pembroke.[3] Sanford turns up again in 1604, when he played an important part in directing Daniel's first masque, *The Vision of the Twelve Goddesses,* presented at Hampton Court. We learn this fact from a letter of 1603 from Sir Thomas Edmonds to Lord Shrewsbury, in whose employ Sanford appears by that time to have been.[4] Sanford wrote a six-line Latin dedication to John Bond's edition of Horace in 1606, and after that we see no more of him except for an allusion in 1621 in John Lane's manuscript poem, *Triton's Trumpet,* that links him and Daniel as "twoe sweetlie-singing swannes of Somerset." [5]

In what might be called the middle period of Daniel's career, 1599 and 1603 marked the publication of new and important work. With 1599 came a fifth book of the *Civil Wars,* with a verse dedication to Mountjoy; a *Letter from Octavia to Marcus Antonius,* dedicated to Lady Margaret, Countess of Cumberland; and *Musophilus,* dedicated to Fulke Greville. From those dedications it is evident that he had been widening his circle of patronage. The days at Wilton were now over, and the poet drew closer to Mountjoy. He must have spent considerable time at the latter's country seat at Wanstead, to which he refers in his work with familiarity and affection. Now, four years after his acknowledgement of Mountjoy's aid in the 1595 *Civil Wars* (1.5), his dedication of the whole volume, *Poetical Essays,* which contained the *Civil Wars,* shows him to be more solidly established in that nobleman's favor. Noticeable are the tone of confidence, the signs of mutual regard between patron and poet, and a characteristic absence of fawning servility:

> I do not plant thy great respected name
> Here in this front, to th'end thou shouldst protect
> These my endevors from contempt or blame,
> Which none but their own forces must effect:
> Nor do I seeke to win thy more respect,
> Most learned Lord, by these Essaies of mine,

> Since that cleere judgment that did first elect
> To favor me will alwaies keepe me thine:
>
> . . . .
>
> But this I do to th'end if destinie
> Shall any monument reserve of me,
> Those times should see my love, how willing I
> That liv'd by thee, would have thee live with me.

This manly tone Daniel continues to sound towards Mountjoy even after the latter's death in 1606. The first period of this association must have lasted from 1594 through 1600, when Mountjoy left on his military expedition to Ireland.

Only a few years after the beginning of Daniel's friendship with Mountjoy came his establishment in the household of the Lady Margaret, Countess of Cumberland. She was a Clifford, and Daniel had already written a celebrated poem about Rosamond Clifford only a few years before. He must have joined Lady Margaret's establishment in 1597 or 1598 when he became tutor to her young daughter Anne (born in 1590), who was later to become Countess of Dorset, Pembroke, and Montgomery. These associations too proved to be of long standing. In 1603 Daniel wrote verse epistles to both mother and daughter, and many years later he wrote Anne a consolatory letter[6] when she was experiencing a very unhappy marriage. He must have instilled in his pupil a life-long regard, for in a "great picture" she had painted in later years she placed his portrait with this inscription below it: "Tutour to this Young Lady, a man of an upright and excellent Spirit, as appeared by his works." [7]

I *The* Letter from Octavia

The *Letter from Octavia* was dedicated to Lady Margaret. A poem of some four hundred lines in ottava rima stanzas, its form is that of the love epistle in verse made popular long before by Ovid in *Epistolae Heroidum,* a work easily accessible to Daniel, either directly in Latin or through a series of translations by Turberville beginning in 1567. Moreover, Drayton in this instance was ahead of Daniel, for he had in 1597 published *England's Heroical Epistles,* an exchange of imaginary letters between such pairs of lovers as King Henry and Rosamond, Edward IV and

Jane Shore, the Earl of Surrey and the Lady Geraldine. Drayton's spirited poems are in rhyming couplet verse. And Samuel Brandon, whose tragedy *The Virtuous Octavia* was modelled after Daniel's *Cleopatra,* also wrote an exchange of epistles between Octavia and Antonius, published along with the tragedy in 1598. Brandon's two poems are in monotonous singsong verse. His Octavia is quite unlike Daniel's; she, vindictive throughout, is armed with her own moral superiority and with the smug assurance that Antony will suffer for his neglect. She lectures him on the price he must pay for his sensuality and indifference, yet she is willing to have him return to her. Brandon's Antony has only slightly more appeal; he is an evasive, cowardly rogue whose lame excuses make him slightly amusing.

Daniel might have read Brandon's poem, but, if he did, he shows no indebtedness. His own poem had been entered in the Stationers' Register early in January, 1599, and a manuscript of it has been found written in the hand of Daniel's good friend and fellow poet, Sir John Harington.[8] The Dedication and the Argument of the printed version are not found in the manuscript, and numerous other textual differences reveal conclusively that the 1599 printed version was considerably revised.[9] Daniel's poem then was written at least as early as 1598.

The dedication to Lady Margaret is significant. She was the daughter of Francis Russell, second Earl of Bedford, and her marriage to George Clifford, third Earl of Cumberland, was as unhappy as Octavia's to Antony. Clifford was often absent from home, and his intrigue with a lady of the court led to separation from his wife.[10] So Daniel chose a traditional story, carrying with it sentiments which would strike a responsive chord in the countess. He was especially gifted in depicting the pathetic aspect of things, and he is usually at his best in presenting afflicted women who conduct themselves with dignity and grace. We find this quality in Rosamond, Cleopatra, Octavia; and we catch some of this spirit in the dedicatory sonnet to Lady Margaret. The poet promises that he will "bestow/Words upon griefe, as my griefes comprehend," and of Octavia he says that he will try to make this "great afflicted Lady show,/Out of my feelings, what she might have pend." The poem itself shows how well Daniel could enter into a woman's feelings and present her point of view.

[82]

We see Octavia in the process of writing her letter while imagining how it will be received by the partially penitent Antony as he proceeds to read it in due time and far away. Although the whole poem consists of the text of her epistle, the early part of it acquires dramatic interest by anticipating scenes and events that lie outside the letter. Throughout the poem (for instance, stanzas 17–19) there is a strong claim for the "best parts" of woman's nature that have been unjustly subdued by man:

> You can be onely heard, whilst we are taught
> To hold our peace, and not to exercise
> The powers of our best parts, because your parts
> Have with our freedome robb'd us of our harts.

Women, Octavia says, have acquired though living in submission a discipline that often provides them with superior insight:

> We, in this prison of our selves confin'd,
> Must here shut up with our owne passions live,
>
> . . . .
>
> Yet oft our narrowed thoughts looke more direct
> Then your loose wisdomes born with wild neglect.

If women, she continues, were as loose in love as men, chaos would come again. Her argument has a familiar modern ring: "What? are these barres for us, no bounds for you?" And her comment (Stanza 21) is like Emilia's in *Othello* (IV.iii.87–102), though quite different in spirit:

> And if we have shut in our hearts from lust,
> Let not your bad example let them out,
> Thinke that there is like feeling in our bloud:
> If you will have us good, be you then good.

One of the paradoxes of man's licentiousness, Ocatavia says, is that it makes women's self-control all the firmer. But she herself has feminine feelings too, and she cannot abide the thought of Cleopatra's supposed scorn. While inviting Antony to return to her, Octavia deplores the strife that is certain to break out between her husband and her brother and make her a loser in any event. She reminds Antony of the disgraceful irony in the world's beholding two great men at odds over two weak women, and she tells him in her suffering of the unwanted pity she gets from others, whereas her only wish is to move him to feel for her.

Toward the end of the poem, Daniel gives an interesting turn to the story. Octavia asks Antony to come back and all will be forgotten; if he does not, then she envisages from a recent dream the horrors to come (stanzas 47–48). In the dream a hippopotamus is floating from the Nile River into the sea with a wanton mermaid on his back "as if she rul'd his course, and steer'd his fate." And then another challenges the hippopotamus, while the mermaid watches the bloody struggle and finally flees from the scene; she is followed by her champion "as if his heart and strength lay in her eyes." This little episode, not related in Plutarch, enlivens a monologue which occasionally lags, by the infusion of an allegory that is prophetic of the defeat at Actium. The mermaid, or siren, traditionally seductive and lustful, appropriately represents Cleopatra. The more usual association with the dolphin is dropped here for the hippopotamus, no doubt because the poet wanted to make more literal Antony's association with the Nile and Egypt. Shakespeare was to present us with still another view of Antony, as Cleopatra figuratively sees him swimming: "His delights/Were dolphin-like, they shew'd his backe above/The Element they liv'd in" (*Antony and Cleopatra*, V.ii.88–90).

A masterful touch is given to Daniel's poem in the second stanza. Octavia's letter to Antony contains, besides her generally challenging reproach to Antony, a sarcastic taunt which she anticipates will come from Cleopatra. And she adds in the following stanza her own reply to the imagined twitting from Egypt's queen. It is as though the women rivals are carrying on a dialogue through a letter addressed to the man.

> Although perhaps, these my complaints may come
> Whilst thou in th'armes of that incestuous Queene,
> The staine of Aegypt, and the shame of Rome
> Shalt dallying sit, and blush to have them seene:
> Whilst proud disdainfull she, gessing from whome
> The message came, and what the cause hath beene,

> Will scorning say, Faith this comes from your Deere,
> Now sir you must be shent for staying heere.
>
> From her indeede it comes, delitious Dame,
> (Thou royall Concubine and Queene of lust)
> Whose armes yet pure, whose breasts are voyde of blame,
> And whose most lawfull flame proves thine unjust:
> Tis she that sends the message of thy shame,
> And his untruth that hath betraid her trust:
> Pardon, deare Lord, from her these sorrowes are,
> Whose bed brings neither infamie nor warre.

Plutarch has no such scene, and it is possible that Shakespeare on reading the poem transferred the mood from Octavia to Cleopatra whom it better suits than it does the sober, dignified Octavia. In a highly effective scene Shakespeare has Cleopatra (instead of Octavia) anticipate Fulvia (in the place of Cleopatra) as taunting Antony (I.i.19–32).[11]

The pace of the *Letter* is almost too leisurely, and the attention lags because the language, though precise, is abstract and colorless. The work has too many smooth connections, too few metaphors. In one sense, it may be seen as a weaker *Rosamond* with a stronger moral intent. Daniel was to do much better in the new kind of poetry he was now undertaking.

II   Musophilus

No poem of Daniel's has won more praise than *Musophilus,* and it remains his most consistently popular work among "the graver sort," to use one of the poet's own expressions. The title describes it as "containing a generall defence of all *learning,*" and the poem does just that. No direct source is known, but Castiglione's *Courtier* is certainly a part of its background. Like the *Courtier, Musophilus* is in dialogue form; in one point at least the two works are alike in arguing for the preeminence of letters over arms.[12] Moreover, "N.W's" prefatory address to Daniel's 1585 translation of Paulus Jovius assumes a close familiarity with Castiglione: "I pray syr, shal *Castilio* be more reverenced for his courtier, then *D. Clarke* admired for investing him with so courtly robes?" [13] This reference is probably to a Latin translation by Bartholomew Clark

in 1571 of the *Courtier* which Daniel must have read, as well as
the original text in Italian and the English translation by Hoby.
Castiglione's book was an influential one with Daniel; it is also in
the background of his later portrait of Devonshire, and it lies too
behind Shakespeare's presentation of Henry V.

Some evidence has been found also for the influence of Montaigne's essays on *Musophilus* and on the later Epistles of 1603.
Daniel probably knew Montaigne in French before he read the
Florio translation in 1603. The conclusion of one writer is that
"enough parallels exist . . . to suggest that the *Essays* may have
warmed and stimulated Daniel's Senecanism." [14] Another possible
source, or "spark," the same writer has found in the fourth Eclogue of Thomas Lodge's *A Fig for Momus* (1595).[15] The Eclogue, addressed to Daniel himself, is in the form of a debate
between a soldier and man of action and a meditative, book-
loving statesman. Lodge remains so neutral that Daniel might
have been influenced to say something more on the subject, as
indeed he does in *Musophilus*.

But no influence on Daniel's poem is stronger than that of Fulke
Greville to whom Daniel dedicated *Musophilus* and whom he
prominently mentions at its very end:

> And if herein the curious sort shall deeme
> My will was caried far beyond my force,
> And that it is a thing doth ill beseeme
> The function of a *Poem,* to discourse:
> Thy learned judgement which I most esteeme
> (Worthy *Fulke Grevil*) must defend this course.
> By whose mild grace, and gentle hand at first
> My Infant Muse was brought in open sight
> From out the darkenesse wherein it was nurst.[16]

A number of suggestions are raised by these lines. Possibly it was
Greville who long before first introduced Daniel to the Wilton
circle and gave him encouragement from the start. And, as Daniel
now moves away from the themes of love, passionate mischance,
and war that pervade his earlier poetry to the grave, the philosophic, and the discursive, he turns for justification to Greville,
who must have many times discussed these matters with Daniel

and who indeed himself wrote a poem, *A Treatie of Humane Learning*, of the same kind.

Greville's *Humane Learning* is not a dialogue or a debate, but a treatise in six-line stanzas rhyming *ababcc*, generally the same pattern Daniel used in *Musophilus*. The work sets out to show how sense, as man's first instructor, appears to free him from deception but in reality deceives him most. The next organ, imagination, too is an untrustworthy power, varying with the individual self. Imagination is not always able to receive what sense reports but only what the affections admit. Hence men's passions and desires cause them to perceive objects that do not come from sense at all. Memory and understanding too are limited by man's fallen nature. Nor are these natural defects in man corrected, as it is supposed, by the sciences and the arts, whose pretensions are not within the reach of imperfect, finite man. This skepticism leads Greville to question logic and philosophy themselves as displays of word-magic, in which the verbalists go on engaging "grammar rules in civill warre." As a consequence, books become vain idols; and the arts too are but idols built upon the false foundation of man's guilt and uncertainty.

The end result is a deep skepticism about the reliability of all speculative knowledge, and Greville, not willing to dismiss the arts and sciences as useless, sees their only true value in practice and action: "For *Sciences* from Nature should be drawne,/As *Arts* from *practice*, never out of Bookes." [17] Greville finds deception in words and books, as Bacon does in his *Advancement of Learning* (1603–1605). To Greville, the chief measure of the value of knowledge is in the ethical (including the political) and the religious life. He is skeptical of abstractions; science and mathematics are useful only so far as they serve the practical ends of living. Such a view is antihumanistic, and, like Montaigne, Greville reveals a certain skeptical turning of the humanist mind upon itself. He lacks the optimism of Bacon and of the new science, as well as the humanist optimism of Daniel, whose view of learning and of books is wholly different. For Daniel books are the sinews and the life-blood of men.

Since none of the dates of composition of Greville's poems are known, we cannot say precisely how his *Humane Learning* affected or was affected by the work of Bacon and Daniel. Greville's most recent editor believes that the poem was written after Bacon's *Advancement* was in manuscript and that Greville and Daniel were likely in contact between 1599 and 1603 when they discussed the subject of learning. *Musophilus* offers enough parallels with *Humane Learning* to suggest that Daniel wrote his poem to counter some of Greville's practical objections to theoretical learning that came through their discussion.[18]

Musophilus, lover of the Muses, is pitted against Philocosmus, Man of the World; and the former must defend from the outset the value and uses of learning. The general movement in the course of Musophilus' speeches is *from* learning and letters and the immortality they confer *to* the role also played by them in society, in the affairs of men. Thus Philocosmus' charge of the *impracticality* of learning is refuted, and Daniel is able to extend the meaning of the contemplative life to the active life.

To Philocosmus' charge that Musophilus' days are spent in the ungainful art of poetry at a time when other delights are required by "this wiser profit-seeking age," he confesses that he loves his art and that the fault is in the times: "And I must not do vertue so much wrong/As love her ought the worse for others crime" (23–24). He prefers "t'have liv'd to be, then to have dyde to have," and he hopes that something of his life will survive, at least for a while: "That all this little All, might not descend/Into the darke a universall pray" (37–38). His is the familiar Renaissance cry for the triumph of Art, however limited in duration, over Time.

But Philocosmus is a powerful adversary. He urges that the learned man, the poet, is ever subject to the attack of the "viperous" critic who can himself supplant the artist in public esteem, and thereby he suggests despair to the conscientious poet now being supplanted by new and practical men. Philocosmus is the artist's own diffident voice.

For Musophilus there is no virtue in ignorance and mere power. Ignorance imitates, lacks self-reliance, and aims only at material things, the acquisition of which does not satisfy but brings decay and ruin. All the proud claims to power and possession have their titles "Written in ice of melting vanitie." Virtue and worth are constant throughout all this change, just as Chaucer has lived on through the vicissitudes of time; indeed, he has wrested time itself "and won upon the mighty waste of daies." We are in the decline of the great cycle he began, but still another one is to be born. As for poetry in any age, Musophilus has this to say:

> For these lines are the vaines, the Arteries,
> And undecaying life-strings of those harts
> That still shall pant . . . .
>
> . . . .
>
> O blessed letters that combine in one
> All ages past, and make one live with all,
> By you we do confer with who are gone,
> And the dead living unto councell call:
> By you th'unborne shall have communion
> Of what we feele, and what doth us befall.
>   (183–85;189–94)

This eloquent assurance should be compared with Milton's later famous definition in *Areopagitica:* "But a good book is the precious life-blood of a master spirit, embalmed and treasured up on purpose to a life beyond life." A few lines further on in *Musophilus* comes an expression of the ideal sought in joining the active life with the pursuit of learning: "What good is like to this,/ To do worthy the writing, and to write/Worthy the reading, and the worlds delight?" (198–200). Musophilus goes far beyond merely replying to his opponent's objections. He exposes the barrenness of the "short-liv'd race" of critics and glances for a moment at the richness and profusion of the Elizabethan Age, whose faults lie in a surfeit of its very virtues. From the whims of this "humorous world" and its mad change of fashions, the poet next allows us to see also the variability of men's religious attitudes.

Amid all this flux in an unstable world, Musophilus urges men of power and authority to hold to a course of knowledge and virtue, which will prevent their setting their hearts on memorials in stone; for these become powerless and speechless in time, as Stonehenge silently bears witness. The Stonehenge passage (337–54) is one of the finest stretches of meditative and elegiac verse in English poetry. Musophilus questions not only Philocosmus but us, Stonehenge, and the whole past:

And whereto serve that wondrous *trophei* now,
That on the goodly plaine neare *Wilton* stands?
That huge domb heap, that cannot tel us how,
Nor what, nor whence it is, nor with whose hands,
Nor for whose glory, it was set to shew
How much our pride mockes that of other lands?

And the "gazing passenger" looks on in wonder, asks many questions of his fellow traveler, "and he knowes nothing." He turns now, looks, sighs, "And in himselfe with sorrow doth complaine/The misery of darke forgetfulnesse." Then, continues Musophilus, "ignorance with fabulous discourse" offers to credulity an explanation shot through with superstition; and Stonehenge gives false evidence against its own trusting builders. The worthies of Classical antiquity succeeded much better through their art and learning in bequeathing to us their achievement in written form.

But Philocosmus in no easy foe. He returns with some hard questions to Musophilus: What assurance do you have for post-humous fame? Can you with this barbarous English tongue do what the ancients did? And how many people, after all, have heard of, or read, even the best English poets, including Sidney and Spenser? Learning itself has been divisive, growing into sects and schools in which the best talents are spent on libels and rhymes; how then in after times is the best to be sorted from this jumble of good and bad? Furthermore, learned men are indecisive and the public requires other skills and graces than the useless ones of the poet. These questions are perennially difficult to answer.

Musophilus, who concedes a great deal to his opponent, grants that the world which accepts humanistic values is small, though size is, in fact, a relative thing. The readers in England are a world, an audience large enough. Indeed, if this audience is reduced to only one, "he is to me a Theater large ynow" (569). And if there is no audience at all, Musophilus still has an answer:

But what if none; it cannot yet undo
The love I beare unto this holy skill:
This is the thing that I was borne to do,
This is my Scene, this part must I fulfill.   (575–79)

And praise is not needed, for virtue needs not to gad about in search of fame nor to prostitute herself to ambition.

The last third of the poem, which concludes Musophilus' long speech, is more tedious and abstract—more in the manner of Greville's *Humane Learning*. Though there are some fine things in this section, stanza seems to spin from stanza with such smoothness that the whole discourse has the appearance of a long sentence without stops. Musophilus admits that learning is weakened by dissension, and he traces the history of the decline of religious awe and reverence to the point where the *"Norman* subleties," of which Daniel is elsewhere suspicious, become the measure of all values. Another difficulty is that too few learned men occupy their rightful posts; if they did, our now "drooping academies" would take heart "And set their bold *Plus ultra* far without/The pillars of those *Axioms* age propounds" (825–26). With this great expansion in learning would come the answer to Philocosmus' earlier question: "To shew true knowledge can both speak and do" (836). Learning would then guide the state, as it partially does even now, since it is often called in to repair the damage wrought by the cunning, practical man.

Musophilus next shows how in worldly affairs learned men are better guides than crafty men, and how the eloquence much despised by Philocosmus is one of the instruments of right action. Therefore, he says, do not condemn "the swelling tide and stream of words." He looks ahead to the time when our "heavenly *Eloquence*" will so perfect men that they may "vent the treasure of our tongue" on strange shores "in th'yet unformed Occident" from which worlds it "may come refin'd with th'accents that are ours." Here is a beautiful prophetic vision of the potential glories of American literature. And Musophilus has the last word about his antagonist's contempt for poetry; numbers, he says, "shew, weakenes speaks in prose, but powre in verse" (980). Daniel turns, in conclusion, for final justification of his poetic undertaking to Fulke Greville.

Musophilus has an elevated theme delivered in appropriate style. Rarely does an undignified line appear in it, and it has some moments of greatness. Sober, serious, and usually eloquent, it sometimes—frequently in the latter part—acquires a tone of unrelieved monotony; and the reader has the feeling that Daniel's style is drawing closer to Greville's, that the metaphors of sense in his earlier work are fading more and more into the abstract figures that abound in Greville. Perhaps Daniel's temperament from the start was more congenial to reflective, restrained verse; and all that was needed to give him more pronounced direction in that kind was the renewed encouragement and possible example of Greville around 1598. There is less emotional impact in the Daniel of this period; but, when strong feeling occurs, as in the Stonehenge passage in *Musophilus*, it has a fine restraint. Hyperbole and rhetoric are avoided, and literal accuracy is sought more than is perhaps necessary.

Daniel's habits of revision may be readily seen in this poem. He so tinkered with the work and excised such large portions of it that the subsequent editions are actually inferior to the first. Part of the difficulty was caused by the poet's uncertainty about the role Greville was to play both in and out of the poem. The 1005 lines of the 1599 poem were reduced to 989 lines in 1601 and then drastically cut to 804 lines in 1607—with deplorable results. Nothing so well illustrates the closely woven fabric of the whole as the poet's failure to detach portions of it successfully from the rest. This is shown in the poet's excision of lines 343–90, the bulk of the great Stonehenge passage, which had movingly described the "gazing passenger" musing over "the misery of darke forgetful-nesse" that time brings, followed by the "fabulous discourse" of ignorance explaining the building of Stonehenge by the myth of how Merlin had brought over the stones and erected them in memory of the Britons treacherously murdered by Hengist. All this, Musophilus had said, is legend; and, inveighing against such ignorance, he had indicted Stonehenge itself for giving false evidence. The omission in 1607 of this indictment of superstitious credulity impairs the poem, for the retained passage that follows represents the "great worthies of antiquitie" as possessing more lasting tombs in the works they have left behind. This section is more effective when set beside the Stonehenge passage of the original version. The later omission of lines 677–790 similarly damages the poem.

III   *The Verse Epistles*

The *Musophilus* and the six verse Epistles of 1603 are the crowning achievements of Daniel as a writer of philosophic verse expressive of the best in Renaissance humanism. The Epistles were all published in the same year as his prose work in criticism, *The Defence of Ryme,* although a reference to them in the *Defence* indicates that the poems were written earlier.[19] The six Epistles, three addressed to men and three to women, are all acknowlege-ments of direct association with powerful and influential person-ages of the day: Sir Thomas Egerton, Lord Keeper of the Great Seal; Lord Henry Howard, of the King's Privy Council; Lady Margaret, Countess of Cumberland; Lady Lucie, Countess of Bedford; Lady Anne Clifford, daughter to Lady Margaret; and Henry Wriothesly, Earl of Southampton. All these poems have a more or less common theme: admiration and respect for the forti-tude that enables the individual to endure injustice and the vicis-situdes of fortune. The qualities extolled are stoic, and the per-sons exhibited are outstanding examples of Classical virtue, firm and enduring. Daniel's work here met with highest praise from such later Romantics as Wordsworth, Hazlitt, and Hartley Cole-ridge.

The well-reasoned Epistle to Egerton is at times an eloquent tribute to equity and to such worthy ministers of it as Egerton himself, who had become Lord Keeper in 1596. The poet sees the ideal role of justice and equity as an isthmus between the two oceans of "Rigor" and confused "Uncertainty." To Egerton, the lawyer, Daniel once again boldly expresses his impatience with the Norman subtleties of the law, which he asserts are more often on the side of wrong than of right. Moreover, they create discord through a war of words growing out of their jargon: "As if it liv'd immur'd within the walls,/Of hideous termes fram'd out of bar-barousnesse/And forraine Customes" (48–50). The true law dwells free in the open plain, "easie of accesse," and unlike intri-cate falsehood, it wears "one face, one colour, one assurednesse." Daniel tactfully reminds Egerton that equity is a "Haven of Peace" that seeks to draw justice from "the tempests of the law" and to "set her in a calme and even way." The more laws, the

more men's actions will circumvent them. Equity, a sanctuary for
the oppressed, is unwritten and relaxed, as opposed to inflexible
law, and it is this instrument that has been committed, he tells
Egerton, "to thy most even and religious hand,/Great Minister of
Justice" (198–99). This argument for simple, direct legal termi-
nology, which may seem naïve, is in harmony with the poet's
view of the English idiom generally. Both *Musophilus* and the
Defence of Ryme express an aversion to wars of words and to
wrangling contention.

This first epistle, in ottava rima stanzas, is the longest of the
group, and it exhibits some of Daniel's limitations as a poet. Too
often intricately and closely reasoned rhymed prose, it displays in
the long sentences that unfold one dependent clause after another,
some of the verbal subtlety that the poet is himself objecting to in
the practice of law. The latter portion of the poem, particularly, as
in *Musophilus*, is too heavily weighted with abstractions that do
not quite palpably emerge. The work succeeds beautifully in one
respect: it manages to show the way to justice without ever appearing to lecture the Lord Keeper on the subject or, on the other
hand, to indulge in fulsome compliment. The secret probably lies
in Daniel's proper subordination of Egerton to his main theme of
equity. The final line of the poem expresses this central meaning:
"Powre may have our knees, but Justice hath our harts."

The shorter Epistle to Lord Howard expresses much the same
idea, but the virtues of simplicity and directness are sought
through character and action, rather than through the ministra-
tion of law and justice. Praise, says the poet, must be deserved, if
it is to be sincere—as seems to be the case in Daniel's modest,
tactful tribute to Howard:

> And though I might commend your learning, wit,
> And happy uttrance, and commend them right,
> As that which decks you much, and gives you grace,
> Yet your cleere judgement best deserveth it,
> Which in your course hath caried you upright,
> And made you to discerne the truest face,
> And best complexion of the things that breed
> The reputation and the love of men.   (11–18)

The compliment shows taste and sincerity in the poet. But it also illustrates the long, circumstantial sentence—the piling up of clause on clause that so often lapses into flatness.

The central idea emerging from this epistle is Daniel's belief in the eventual triumph of honesty, itself ever plain and direct, as opposed to devious cunning. The notion that even the common, ignorant man can see through deceit is fittingly expressed:

> And be it, that the vulgare are but grosse
> Yet are they capable of truth, and see,
>
> . . . .
>
> And wholy never can deluded be,
> All may a few, few cannot all deceive.   (65–66,69–70)

To the Lady Margaret, a noble poem expressing lofty ideals, contains variations on the central theme of the epistles. The beauty of the virtuous life and mind is set forth with the assurance of its triumph over material power. Much of the success of this poem lies in the aptness of the metaphors and in the consistency with which they are sustained. It begins with "He that of such a height hath built his mind," and it develops the metaphor of a habitation for the virtuous mind—one which must be placed high. Neither fear nor hope can enter this stronghold from which vantage-point the mind can look down on a stormy, insecure world that in its moral madness completely misunderstands itself. This lack of self-knowledge in a chaotic world dominated by passion is beautifully realized in the poem by a series of fine oxymorons: "Where honor, power, renowne/are onely gay afflictions, golden toyle" (15–16). The wars of the mightiest monarchs are but "stately robberies." The house thus becomes a kind of symbol for stoic calm in the midst of turbulence. And the truly ethical man sees the misdirected Pompeys of this world inducing justice to conspire with power and thus convincing themselves that right is as manifold as man's passions. Yet it is not so. All this self-deception comes to nothing. The virtuous man, on the other hand, is not cowed by power and cruelty: "Nor is he moov'd with all the thunder crackes/Of Tyrants threats, or with the surly brow/Of power" (36–38). Though he feels pity for all this ignorance and subsequent distress in those who "still beget/affliction upon im-becilitie," he looks upon it as from a distant shore and with "un-wet eye."

At this point the Countess of Cumberland is brought skillfully into the poem. The poet turns to the countess with "Thus, Mad-ame, fares the man that hath prepar'd/A rest for his desires" (60–61); and he then summarizes what has been learned from the "booke of man/full of the notes of frailtie." The wise man has compared "the best of glory with her sufferings." Such a man, says the poet to the countess, aims at that high eminence; setting his thought near "his glorious mansion," he is firm against the pas-sion and flux of the world, ever true to himself. Man's heart is the center of his world, and he must perfect himself in order to tran-scend his mere animal human nature: "And that unlesse above himselfe he can/Erect himselfe, how poore a thing is man? (98–99).

This concord of "a wel-tun'd minde" is made indestructible by the hand of heaven. The poem ends in tribute to the solid achievement of erecting a virtuous life; its light is focused on the countess; and its last two lines beautifully illuminate the moral contrasts that have been held before us:

> You that have built you by your great desarts,
> Out of small meanes, a farre more exquisite
> And glorious dwelling for your honoured name
> Then all the gold of leaden mindes can frame.

Of almost equal poetic merit is the following epistle *To the Lady Lucie, Countesse of Bedford,* written in terza rima stanza. It was to Lucy, patroness of Jonson and Drayton as well, that Daniel later dedicated his first masque, *The Vision of the Twelve God-desses,* within a year's time of this epistle. Befitting a woman who was so much a friend and favorer of poets, the epistle is a tribute to learning and to books as they contribute to the virtuous life. The first twenty-eight lines are a beautiful development of the building metaphor in which the poet, while admitting that virtue is the same whether she be with those of high or low estate, grace-fully looks towards the countess and her station in saying that virtue is more powerful when she has larger room in which to

operate. The countess and virtue are of the same noble rank, and
the poet effects between them a kind of mutual interchange of
residence, with advantages to both: "And therefore well did your
high fortunes meete/With her, that gracing you, comes grac't
thereby" (26–27). In a sense, each is the other's habitation.

The poet further encourages the young woman to cultivate the
mind by assuring her that true glory comes through study and
learning which—and the note is refreshingly modern—serve as
the key to unlock the prison of her sex. Thereby she will be set
free from weakness and admitted to that enlightened vision—one
we have already met in the virtuous man of the preceding epistle
—of a vain, rolling world of disturbances. It is as if she is to be
admitted to the company of the world's wisest men.

All good, says the poet, comes from the mind which alone is
ours. All else is from without and is subject to the will and whim
of others: "And that unlesse we finde us all within,/We never can
without us be our owne" (62–63). For, in such a case, our very
life is "but a possession held for others use." So much do we grant
ourselves to others' use that we dissemble and counterfeit our
hearts; we set a "shining face" on a "clowdie hart" as if art, not
nature, had made us. The true self is mind. Although books, it is
admitted, cannot *make* the mind, they can "rectify" it by turning
it toward judgment, and thus bring us closer to truth. The epistle
comes to an end with the assurance that the countess is on a
course, *learning,* which runs "the rightest way/That is on Earth."

Most affectionate in tone of all these poems is the one to the
Lady Anne Clifford to whom Daniel had recently been tutor. She
was thirteen years old when the poem was published, and it has
the note of affection and respect which we might expect to find in
a strong relationship between teacher and pupil. But, along with
these qualities, the lines have an artfully managed preceptive content which emphasizes the importance of the young lady's carefully guarding her virtue and chastity in a way befitting the honor
of such a worthy family as hers.

A soft sonnet-like opening suggests the freshness of youth and
innocence in this young girl: "Unto the tender youth of those faire
eyes/ The light of judgement can arise but new,/ And yong the
world appears t'a yong conceit." Then comes a charming picture
of the advantages of the girl's birth and of her well-furnished

mind that has no room for storing other images than those of purity. Allusion is made to her mother, the Lady Margaret, who having brought forth such a comely body in her daughter, has labored to adorn "that better parte, the mansion of your minde" in order to "set your vertues equall to your kinde."

And now, as the mother is introduced, the poet deftly withdraws for the moment as preceptor; he puts the mother in that role by resorting to the device, "she tells you." Honor, "she tells you too," is bounded and must be carefully kept from straying into vulgar ways. The young woman must hold to that proper course and order which she has sought, and then men will seek out *her* region and orb. The lower regions of the moral world, as we have heard Daniel say so many times before, are in confusion. Honor, on the other hand, is derived from the heavenly order itself, so that the young lady must seek the moral height that befits her sphere. She must not presume on her rank, but she also must not distrust herself. She should beware self-flattery, for the enemy is both without and within—and even her own heart can ambush her. The poem finally concentrates all this advice on honor upon the quiet, institutional demand of family and marriage: she must convey the "honourable bloud" of Clifford and Russell to a posterity that will be proud of such an upright family. Learning and virtue could be directed to no finer human end.

The final epistle, addressed to Henry Wriothesley, Earl of Southampton, is somewhat different from the others both in subject and in the occasion that prompted it. Southampton, who had been drawn into the Essex conspiracy, had stood trial and been imprisoned for two years. Set free by the king in April, 1603, his release is celebrated by Daniel who also pays tribute to his character. Here again we find stoic emphasis on the disciplined character, often set off from the crowd; but, whereas the central person in the other poems has, by cultivation of mind, withdrawn to a vantage point where he witnesses the confusion of the world, we now have the virtuous man engaged in action. Placed in the midst of confusion, cruelty, suffering, he yet rises above it. As a consequence, the poem to Southampton has more vigor, restlessness, and abruptness in its movement than the others. A glance at the opening lines of the first five stanzas makes the point clear:

(1) He who hath never warr'd with misery.
. . . .
(2) The world had never taken so full note.
. . . .
(3) *Mutius* the fire, the torturs *Regulus.*
. . . .
(4) Not to b'unhappy in unhappinesse.
. . . .
(5) How could we know that thou could'st have indur'd.

We do not have in these lines the smooth, colorless connectives that abound in both *Musophilus* and the other epistles. The meter too is rougher, more irregular.

The recurring notion in this well-unified poem is that the best people, the worthiest, are those willing to bear up against fortune and distress. Only trial under the severest conditions is the test of virtue, for then men's otherwise concealed best parts are drawn out. The crown of man's achievement is suffering: "Not to b'unhappy is unhappinesse/And miserie not 'have knowne misery" (29–30). And the allusion to Southampton himself seems clear enough:

> How could we know that thou could'st have indur'd
> With a reposed cheere, wrong and disgrace,
> And with a heart and countenance assur'd
> Have lookt sterne Death, and Horror in the face?   (37–40)

The metaphors play variations on the constant theme: only the tempest shows the seaman's cunning; the man whose conscience assures him that he acts from good motives occupies a high eminence from which he looks not on his own sufferings but at their causes in others.

This poem, as well as others by Daniel, owes much in thought and mood to Seneca, whose moral essay, *De Constantia Sapientis* he apparently had read and thoroughly absorbed. Seneca's character of the wise man calm in storm, the type of Stoic fortitude, is echoed in the later tribute to the Earl of Devonshire, who also is above the reach of fear and evil. The whole thought behind the epistle to Wriothesley, that adversity is the test of character, is a familiar idea that had been given great prominence in Seneca's essay from which the poet is said to have later translated a large portion of his letter written to a "worthy Countesse." [20] In *De Providentia* Seneca offers his stock patterns of virtue: *"Ignem experitur in Mucio, paupertatem in Fabricio, exilium in Rutilio, tormenta in Regulo, venenum in Socrate, mortem in Catone. Magnum exemplum nisi fortuna non invenit."* [21] The rhetorical pattern in the Southampton poem resembles Seneca's:

> *Mutius* the fire, the torturs *Regulus,*
> Did make the miracles of Faith and Zeale:
> Exile renown'd, and grac'd *Rutilius:*
> Imprisonment, and Poyson did reveale
> The worth of *Socrates: Fabricius*
> Povertie did grace that Common-weale
> More then all *Syllaes* riches got with strife,
> And *Catoes* death did vie with *Caesars* life.   (21–28)

Another point in which Daniel is akin to Seneca is his sympathy toward women. Professor Martha Shackford has called attention to Daniel's interest in the feminine points of view of Delia, Rosamond, and Cleopatra, who represent the Renaissance, the Middle Ages, and Classical antiquity, respectively.[22] To this roll of fair women might be added the various ladies affectionately addressed in the epistles, as well as the outraged Octavia pleading her case for injured womanhood, and finally the virtuous and charming Lady Grey of the *Civil Wars.* Daniel's is often the feminine way of looking at a question, and it suits well with the Stoic tendency to regard women as the equals of men.

IV   *Literary Criticism:* The Defense of Ryme

Daniel's masterpiece in literary criticism, *A Defence of Ryme,* appeared in 1603 as a reply to a lively little essay of the year before, *Observations in the Art of English Poesie,* by the poet and composer Thomas Campion, who reopened the case for quantitative verse in English some twenty years after it had been discussed and experimented with in the circle of Sidney, Spenser, and Dyer. The cause had been a dying one although Campion himself wrote some fine quantitative verse.

In this essay Campion does not insist on the unqualified superiority of quantitative over accentual verse.[23] He begins by saying that "in a verse the numeration of the syllables is not so much to be observed as their weight and due proportion." Campion would regard "due proportion" in the musical sense of syllable length. The Greeks and Romans, he says, diligently observed quantity in both poetry and prose; and the Renaissance restored the Latin tongue, redeeming it "out of the hands of the illiterate monks and friars." In those "lack-learning" times rhyme and meter, now used generally in Christendom, had its beginnings.

Campion has a sensitive ear and many of his observations are ingenious, as when he says that one of the limitations of rhyme is that it oftentimes forces a man "to abjure his matter, and extend a short conceit beyond all bounds of art." Campion's attack on the Procrustean writers of quatorzains, who force the syllables, stretching and contracting them, is particularly effective. He examines the possibilities of the various kinds of metrical feet in English poetry and finds the Latin dactyl not suitable. His analysis of the iambic measure is masterly. In short, his discussion is sensitive and ingenious; but his fresh and chatty tone is somewhat bumptious and annoyingly authoritative. Not only his attack on rhyme but also his contemptuous attitude toward the Middle Ages prompted Daniel's reply. Campion had shown a brash arrogance in both his literary and historical attitudes, and Daniel's *Defence* goes beyond the discussion of the technicalities of rhyme to the verdict of history.

Daniel, whose essay begins with a short Preface "to all the Worthie Lovers and learned Professors of Ryme," explains that about a year earlier he had written a private letter to a great friend of his in court (possibly Fulke Greville) setting forth his ideas on rhyme, which he has since expanded into the *Defence* for publication under the patronage of the Earl of Pembroke. The whole *Defence* that follows is addressed to Pembroke and hence should be regarded as epistolary in form.

With candid self-analysis, the poet confesses that the most "apparent" faults of his nature are irresolution and self-distrust; but in this case, where his professional station as a poet is threatened, he is resolved to defend it. He shows clearly what has most offended him in Campion's essay when he says: "We could well have allowed of his numbers had he not disgraced our Ryme;

Which both Custome and Nature doth most powerfully defend, Custome that is before all Law, Nature that is above all Arte. Every language hath her proper number or measure fitted to use and delight." [24] From this statement we know that Daniel is going to place his discussion of rhyme within the larger context of history.

He proceeds to the discussion of rhyme, which consists of "an agreeing sound in the last silables of severall verses, giving both to the Eare an Eccho of a delightfull report & to the Memorie a deeper impression of what is delivered therein." He cites the prevalence of rhymes in countries beyond western Europe: Turkey, Arabia, Hungary, Russia. And from this fact he sees in it "an hereditary eloquence proper to all mankind" which from its universality argues its general power. True number, measure, and eloquence are to be judged by whatever force of words move, delight, and sway man's affections. Daniel implies that there is no established universal form of poetry.

What, he asks, will be gained by giving up rhyme? And in witty word-play unusual in him, he replies that poets will merely put off these fetters to receive others, for it is "as good still to use ryme and a little reason, as neither ryme nor reason." He refuses to regard the Greek and Latin poets as infallible. They too exhibit many stylistic faults, "and when you finde them disobedient to their owne Lawes, you must hold it to be *licentia poetica,* and so dispensable." The ancients, particularly in their odes, are unnecessarily intricate; and Daniel's characteristic impatience with subtleties and complications, whether in law or in poetry, again comes to the fore. There seems, he says, to be a general presumption among men that "every science, every profession, must be so wrapt up in unnecessary intrications as . . . to confound the understanding." It is "as if Art were ordained to afflict Nature." Daniel is consistent in this attitude toward all intricacy, even in the making of rhyme itself, which he is so seriously defending here. He expresses a dislike for a wide variety of rhymes, especially as they appear in sonnet writing. His own rhyme schemes, as we have seen, are neither widely varied nor intricate as a rule; and in this respect he is in sharp contrast with both Spenser and Sidney whom he so highly regarded.

Rhyme, instead of being an impediment to the imagination, as

Campion had said, provides the poet with wings, carrying him "to a farre happier flight." Daniel very clearly sees the disciplinary value of rhyme, particularly in the sonnet; it operates on the chaos of passion by imposing finite form upon the infinite, the whole being "excellently ordered in a small roome." Wordsworth was later to echo the phrase in "the sonnet's scanty room," and both he and Coleridge were to say much the same thing about the function of rhyme. The moderns, says Daniel, by using the stanza of six, seven, or eight lines (which predominate in his own compositions), are able to establish the movement of the whole but to keep it within the measure of a "just period." Classical writers, on the other hand, run on and on, only to confound the reader, who must go back "to retrive the escaped sence."

Daniel returns to the assault on Campion's claim of the supremacy of the ancients. He drives home his main point in a ringing, clear, and eloquent prose style, one unrivaled in his time:

All our understandings are not to be built by the square of *Greece* and *Italie*. We are the children of nature as well as they, we are not so placed out of the way of judgment, but that the same Sunne of Discretion shineth uppon us. . . . All their Poesie, all their Philosophie is nothing, unlesse we bring the discerning light of conceipt with us to apply it to use. It is not bookes, but onely that great booke of the world, and the all-overspreading grace of heaven that makes men truely judiciall. Nor can it be but a touch of arrogant ignorance, to hold this or that nation Barbarous, these or those times grosse, considering how this manifold creature man, wheresoever hee stand in the world, hath alwayes some disposition of worth.[25]

And if China has never heard of anapests and trochees, can men justly call them gross and barbarous?

Almost directly quoting Campion's claim that, after the Roman empire, Europe passed through "lack-learning" times until the coming of the Renaissance humanists, Daniel shows that learning never died and that there was admirable achievement in literature through the Middle Ages too. He shows a wide, profound reading in medieval and Renaissance literature: Petrarch, Tasso, Aretino, Gaza, Reuchlin, Moore, Bede, Walter Map, Bacon, Occam—to name only a few. Daniel's argument carries with it the ever necessary reminder in all ages that wisdom and great achievement are not the exclusive possession of one's own time or of some far-off golden age of the past. Brash ignorance needs to be told this fact over and over again: "So that it is but the clowds gathered about our owne judgement that makes us thinke all other ages wrapt up in mists, and the great distance betwixt us, that causes us to imagine men so farre off, to be so little in respect to our selves." [26] England, he says, is not any more the product of the Renaissance than of the Middle Ages. To establish the quality of men and societies requires a long time.

Another thing that has irked Daniel about Campion is that the latter has provided only a few loose, facetious epigrams to illustrate the poetry he advocates, instead of offering examples of merit. At this point Daniel presents a detailed analysis of Campion's essay, and his remarks are acid. First, Daniel says, we must, according to the "Adversary" whom he never names, imitate the ancients, and then we are shown how to disobey them. We are told, in short, all the advantages and values of ancient verse, and then we are shown how much of it is not suited to English. And the world will hardly subscribe to the authority of this law-giving Campion, this *Radamanthus* who tortures syllables. Campion would bring words into obedience, by arbitrary tyranny. But what is to prevent other tyrannies to follow? Though he has sometimes been called a forerunner of English neo-Classicism, Daniel here is solidly English in his rejection of academicism in letters.

Daniel concludes from Campion's own principles and examples that what finally emerges as usable are English verse forms already in use for a long time. He next questions what motives had led Campion to make his proposals. It could have been neither for the learned, who would have had no need of such obvious information, nor for the ignorant (and here Daniel wittily turns one of Campion's own contemptuous phrases, "fat Ryme," against him), who on becoming versifiers would give us "leane Numbers, instede of fat Ryme." He can only conclude, then, that Campion's purpose was to show his own skill, and, in the course of it all, do wrong to the dead, to the living, and to England.

Daniel's tone now becomes less harsh and combative as he modestly acknowledges the limitations of traditional English verse and rhyme. Though he would not undertake to instruct others, couplets, he says, by their frequency and certainty eventually become tiresome. Blank verse, especially in tragedy, has considerable merit—a concession to Campion. Daniel says, as we know from his works, that he most favors alternating or "cross" rhymes, with some variations. He eschews the mixing of masculine and feminine rhymes, "holding feminine Rymes to be fittest for Ditties"; but he does not insist that others avoid them. In his discussion of the faults to which poets are prone, his account of their self-love and consequent blindness anticipates the self-love with which Alexander Pope later charged critics; and we can almost hear the voice of Pope himself here and a little further on in Daniel's essay where affectation is singled out as another fault. But the whole matter, Daniel liberally concedes as he comes to an end, is to be left to time and to custom.

The *Defence* is marked by its moderation and good sense, by its weighty and vigorous prose style. In this fine expression of Classic objectivity, we are taken to a height, through the controversy's being placed in history, from which we can perceive the limited dimensions of the technical quarrel itself. The thing that matters is that, if we recognize our limited judgment in a world of change, it is ridiculous to impose our dogmatic notions on others. Yet it should be recognized that Daniel's tone is at times angry, at least nettled, and that this usually peace-loving, diffident man occasionally displays a tart and mocking irony. Perhaps much of the impassioned tone of the whole work comes from a man who has been personally hurt and whose craft is in question.

V *Summary: Daniel's Transition to New Interests*

Within the short space from 1598 to 1603 Daniel produced a considerable amount of verse and prose in a mode new for him; mainly ethical and critical in inspiration and thought, it was epistolary in form. A convergence of influences—from Seneca, Montaigne, Castiglione, and Fulke Greville—pushed him toward versifying moral philosophy, but perhaps his interest lay here from the start. There seem to have been very little turbulence and impetuosity in Daniel. The exuberant and the voluptuous are seldom if ever found in his creations. Those qualities which we like to associate with him, calm, fairness, modesty, love of learning—in short, the concord of the well-tuned mind—find their most concentrated expression in *Musophilus,* in the *Defence,* and in the verse epistles. Set beside the more youthful *Delia, Musophilus* and the epistles reveal a far more mature poet.

This period of Daniel's literary activity ends with the death of Elizabeth in 1603. He had already been forming new allegiances since 1600, and he now sought to win favor with James I. He was soon to return to the drama, though to drama of a different sort, and he was composing and revising a variety of larger and smaller works during the period 1600–1606.

CHAPTER 6

New Associations and Changing Fortunes
(1601-1606)

WHEN the end of the century found Daniel's literary reputation well established, he was living in the households of the Countess of Cumberland and of Lord Mountjoy. His dedications addressed to various persons of power and influence during this period are proof that he had come under the notice of a growing number of helpful patrons. Although the tradition that Queen Elizabeth appointed Daniel "lauriate" on the death of Spenser in 1599 is extremely doubtful, we need not infer that he did not enjoy her patronage. The 1601 *Civil Wars* is dedicated to Elizabeth whom the poet calls "happier then all thy great Progenitors,/ That ever sate upon that powerfull throne." And in this dedication Daniel is clearly acknowledging receipt of material support from the queen:

> I, who by that most blessed hand sustain'd
> In quietnes, doe eate the bread of rest:
> And by that all-reviving powre obtain'd,
> That comfort which my Muse and me hath blest.

Long afterward, in 1609, six years after the queen's death, his opening lines of the *Civil Wars* again allude to her favor: "On yet, sad Verse: though those bright starres, from whence/ Thou hadst thy light, are set for evermore."

I *Testimonials to Authors, Patrons, and Friends*

That Daniel had won the notice of Sir Thomas Egerton, Lord Keeper of the Great Seal, we know from the epistle addressed to him in 1603. Egerton's patronage was sought by many writers. He was a benefactor of Oxford University and became its chancellor in 1610. His love of learning is attested by his great collection of books and manuscripts at Ashridge. When Egerton was created

Lord Ellesmere, the collection was so named for him and later became known as the Bridgewater collection. Among the authors he favored with patronage were Sir John Davies, John Davies of Hereford, Francis Thynne, and Daniel. The relationship between Daniel and the Lord Keeper is also shown by an undated letter, probably of 1602, which the poet attached to a gift copy for Egerton of the 1601 *Works*.[1]

The letter opens on a note of thankfulness: "Amongst all the great workes of your Worthynes, it will not be the least that you have donne for me in the preferment of my brother, with whome yet now sometimes I may eat, whilst I write, and so go on with the worke I have in hand, which God knowes, had long since been ended, and your Honour had had that which in my haste I have prepared for you, could I have but sustayned myself and made truce within, and peace with the world. But such hath been my misery, that whilst I should have written the actions of Men, I have been constrayned to live with children, and contrary to myne owne Spirit, putt out of that scene, which nature had made my parte." [2]

From this statement we may gather that Egerton had given substantial aid to the poet's younger musician-brother John, which help in turn greatly benefitted Daniel himself as he pushed on with his *Civil Wars*. John, born in Someretshire around 1565, had attended Christ Church College, Oxford, where he took the degree of Bachelor of Music on July 14, 1600. He is generally regarded as a musician and composer of importance. The dates of the letter and of the degree indicate that the musician, only recently from the university, may have needed the advancement and encouragement such a man as Egerton could give him. The poet is apologizing to Egerton for his long delay in bringing the *Civil Wars* to an end, and the wording suggests that he felt under considerable obligation, perhaps in the form of a promise, to the Lord Keeper for finishing it; if so, then Egerton may have become his patron much earlier. In the remark about living with children, Daniel probably alludes to his tutorship of Ann Clifford, which apparently was continuing in 1602. He will be happy, he says further, if he can bring his history down to the time of Henry Tudor; it would be the end of his "ambition in this life, and the utmost" of his desires. So dedicated is he to his task that, he adds, "I purpose to retyre me to my pore home, and not again to see you 'till I have payed your Honour my vowes."

The poet paid tribute in verse to still other friends and associates. Especially appropriate in spirit and language is his ninety-line dedication of another copy of the 1601 volume to Sir Thomas Bodley, founder of the famous library named for him at Oxford. He praises the wisdom of Bodley, feels gratitude that his book has found "a little roome" in this "goodly Magazine of witte," and goes on to show how material things pass from hand to hand and are never permanently man's; they are only gifts which fortune takes back and redistributes. But books, which are for the common good, are permanently the possession of all. The library, he says, immures "the glorious reliques of the best of men" and its purpose is thus given:

> For this is to communicate with men
> That good the world gave by societie,
> And not like beasts of prey, draw all to our Den
> T'inglut our selves, and our owne progenie.[3]

"Discreet Antiquitie," the poet says, erected "an everlasting Granery of Artes" to feed the state. Every child, if he is "borne unto Letters," is free to claim his share; and the "happy walls" of this library "harbour all commers." This love of learning and this assurance of the permanence of ideas as distinguished from the evanescence of things are in the same spirit we find in *Musophilus* and in several of the Epistles, especially in the one to Lucy.

About the same time Daniel addressed prefatory lines to two new translations, the first of which was an anonymous rendition of Guarini's *Pastor Fido* by a kinsman of Edward Dymoke's. This poem and Tasso's *Aminta* in the original Italian had both been printed for the first time in England in 1591. Daniel no doubt read these authors shortly thereafter, and he must have looked forward with pleasure to the 1602 translation of *Pastor Fido* by a former friend. Within a few years he was himself to write pastoral dramas which go back to Tasso and Guarini as models. We know from the lines that Dymoke, to whom this sonnet is addressed, highly esteemed Guarini, that the translator took great pains and industry in his work, and that Guarini "now in England can/

Speake as good English as Italian." Then the lines suggest that both Dymoke and Daniel had once met Guarini who spoke in disparagement of the "North," [4] which Daniel was always so eager to defend.

The other poem of about ninety lines was addressed in 1603 to his "deere friend" John Florio and was prefaced to the latter's translation of Montaigne's *Essays*. In this preface Daniel says some fine things about Montaigne, but questions at the same time the value of the making of many books. It would seem that the Daniel of *Musophilus*, who was so confident and so optimistic about the knowledge from books, had by 1603 come around, for a moment at least, to a more skeptical view, one nearer to the Fulke Greville of *Humane Learning* or to Montaigne himself. In the opening lines Daniel is far away from *Musophilus:*

> Bookes the amasse of humors, swolne with ease,
> The Griefe of peace, the maladie of rest;
> So stuffe the world, falne into this disease,
> As it receives more then it can digest.[5]

He finds no end to words; they are like the ocean without shore, "as if man labor'd with himselfe to be/ As infinite in words, as in intents." So that the leaves of books are witnesses of our defects more than of our achievement and "this *Babel* of our skill, this *Towre* of wit" may lead us to doubt our knowledge and to guess that "truth hath other shapes then one." We are made aware through the poem that we never quite hit the center of truth. Montaigne, however, does it superbly:

> Which to discover this great Potentate,
> This Prince *Montaigne* (if he be not more)
> Hath more adventur'd of his owne estate
> Then ever man did of himselfe before.

Daniel was one of the first to perceive the unique quality of Montaigne: his search within, his self-exploration and consequent self-revelation, his adventuring "of his own estate." Montaigne's had been a bold attack on custom which Daniel calls "the mightie tyrant of the earth,/ In whose *Seraglio* of subjection/ We all seem bred-up, from our tender birth."

So Daniel stands in admiration "at Montaigne's gate," and he is glad to be "so neere to him whom I do so much love." And now he turns to the translator with a graceful compliment, saying that Florio has "Plac'd him in the best lodging of our speach,/ And made him now as free, as if borne here." Excellence is never destined to die obscure, and it is "the portion of a happie Pen/ Not to b'invassal'd to one Monarchie." Montaigne's book has rich pieces, "though in a troubled frame confus'dly set." Without such a book, says the poet, the richest library can be but poor. Whatever his current skepticism about books, Daniel withdraws it in the case of Montaigne.

II *The Panegyric on King James*

With the death of Elizabeth in the spring of 1603 came moments of anxiety until the new King James began the procession from Scotland southward, stopping for entertainment at various places along the way. Daniel did not join in writing a song of mourning for the departed queen, and Henry Chettle's pastoral, *England's Mourning Garment*, chides him, as well as Drayton, Warner, Jonson, Chapman, and Shakespeare, for their silence; he addresses Daniel as "Thou sweetest song-man of all English swaines." [6] However, Daniel composed for the incoming king a fairly long panegyric of seventy-two ottava rima stanzas. Not a lively poem, it is occasionally even dull, though always sensible. The panegyric never becomes so fulsome and tasteless as Drayton's *The Majesty of King James*, or as John Seville's effusive *Salutatory Poem to the Majesty of King James*, or as a number of other such pieces on this occasion. Daniel appears to have hurried north with his poem to meet the king, and it is likely that Lucy, Countess of Bedford, arranged for the meeting at Burleigh Harrington. She herself had quickly won the new king's favor and had then escorted Queen Anne to England. [7] At any rate, the title page of Daniel's poem reads in part: "A Panegyrike Congratulatorie Delivered to the Kings Most Excellent Majestie at Burleigh Harrington in Rutlandshire. By Samuel Daniel." In the printed issues and editions of 1603 the poem was accompanied by the *Epistles* and by the *Defence of Ryme*. It would be interesting to know in what form Daniel delivered his panegyric to the king.

The poem, entered on the Stationers' Register on May 30, 1603, could have reached printed form in early June. But it was "delivered" when the king was at Burleigh, April 24 to 26, and therefore was probably read from a manuscript copy. Such a copy, containing fifty-eight of the seventy-three stanzas, exists;[8] and it is written throughout in what looks like Daniel's script.[9] The differences in reading, as well as the omissions in the manuscript, clearly indicate that it is an earlier version of the poem upon which the printed texts are based; and it is likely, therefore, that at Burleigh Daniel read from it or another manuscript copy.

The poet greets the incoming king with the highest praise, reviewing a family background—the descent from Henry VII through the marriage of Margaret of Richmond to Scotland's James IV—that insures the union of all Britain. The poem nicely mixes eulogy with some seasonable advice. Daniel tactfully lectures the king on what he is to do and on what he should avoid doing. The advice is gracefully offered with the air of assurance that the king *will* do the right thing: he will of course be fair to all alike; be above bribery, corruption, mean revenge, and extortion; and not surround himself with flatterers and countenance a licentious court. Instead, he will foster justice and honesty; and avoiding innovation, he will continue in the great tradition from which he has come. Though sluggish in movement and stuffed with the gathering abundance of abstractions found elsewhere in Daniel's work of this period, the poem shows courage, honesty, and tact. In one instance, stanza nine, the king is gently but firmly reminded:

> Whereby, O mighty Soveraigne, thou art tolde
> What thou and thine are likely to expect
> From such a faith, that doth not haste to runne
> Before their time to an arising Sunne.[10]

The dignity and the self-respect with which Daniel addresses noblemen are retained when he faces the king.

Stanzas fifty-two and fifty-three are addressed to the poet's own muse. He is reminded now of how the new king is bringing peace and concord, just as the illustrious Henry VII had done more than a hundred years before. And this thought leads him to regret that he himself has failed to bring his tale of "bloudy warre into a quiet bed." He had expressed similar regret and dissatisfaction with himself in his letter to Egerton the year before. To the muse he promises that she shall "have the benefite/ Of quietnesse which thou hast wanted long." Six years later he ceased all work on the *Civil Wars*.

One interesting feature of the manuscript version is the light thrown on Sir Walter Ralegh at one of the most critical moments of his life. In stanza thirty-five of the manuscript Daniel is reminding the king that there are other riches and dignities than material wealth: "By which improvement we shall gaine much more/ Than b'all *Guiana*, all Discoveries." In all the printed versions of 1603 the second line here reads: "Then by *Peru* or all discoveries"—a revision that is highly suggestive. Ralegh had sailed from England early in 1595; on his return the following year, he had published his *Discoverie of Guiana*. Though an enemy of Essex at the time of the latter's trial in 1601, he apparently did not plot, as some maintained, against Essex' life, while remaining loyal to the queen. When James of Scotland was informed that Ralegh was opposed to his own claims to the throne, he felt strong hostility toward him as he came southward in the spring of 1603. Ralegh, upon hearing rumors about his impending dismissal from the office of Captain of the Guard, could bear the suspense no longer and set out to meet the king, in spite of the latter's proclamation that was intended to stop him.[11] When he met James at Burleigh House sometime between April 23 and 26, he was coldly received; and tradition has it that the king curtly addressed him with "I have heard but rawly of thee." Quickly dismissed by James, Ralegh was relieved a short time later of the captaincy.

Ralegh then was at Burleigh Harrington at the very time Daniel presented his *Panegyrike*. What lies behind Daniel's revision of the passage, substituting the allusion to Drake for the one to Ralegh? It isn't likely that we will ever know for certain. But we may venture a guess. Drake had died in 1596 (the year Ralegh's book had appeared), and twenty years lay behind that date and his earlier seizure of American, including Peruvian, treasure. He was already a part of England's glorious past and his name, as Daniel must suddenly have become aware, was far safer to imply than Ralegh's. We do not know why the allusion to Ralegh appeared in Daniel's manuscript poem in the first place. We have no proof that they ever met, though we do know that Ralegh had read Daniel. In his *History of the World* (entered in 1611 and published in 1614) Ralegh reviews the story of Philotas, which Daniel had made into a tragedy published in 1605, and then he turns to "a poet of our own," quoting the first fourteen lines of the chorus from Act III of Daniel's play.[12] Perhaps earlier enthusiasm for Ralegh led Daniel to put the great voyager into his poem; but, confronted with Ralegh's fast-waning popularity, he acted with characteristic caution—or possibly even out of concern for Ralegh's own safety—in taking him out of the poem. It seems likely that he made this particular change shortly before the poem was "presented," around April 25.

The 1603 volume containing the *Panegyrike,* the *Epistles,* and the *Defence* also included a curious poem of indifferent merit, "The passion of a distressed man," which presents a man's debating with himself, alone in a boat at sea with two women, as to how he shall carry out Neptune's orders to cast out one of them, either the loved and disdainful woman or the loving and scorned one. First the distressed man would cast away the faithful damsel, and then he reasons that he should consign himself and both women to the sea. Finally, he decides to sacrifice the disdainful one. Sir John Harington, Daniel's admiring friend and the translator of Ariosto, also wrote a poem on the same subject, which affords a kind of moral and literary exercise.[13] In two recorded copies of the Daniel volume an extra leaf without signature is inserted; it contains a prose epistle to the Earl of Hertford "concerning his question of a distressed man," etc.; and it makes clear that the subject was first proposed to Daniel by the nobleman. The extra leaf might have been inserted later than 1603, after Daniel had met the Earl of Hertford, who, because of a rival claim to the succession, had been persecuted under Elizabeth and had only gradually been restored to prestige and favor after the accession of James in 1603. Hertford appears later in 1608 as a probable friend and benefactor of the poet.[14]

III *The First Masque*

On January 8, 1604, Daniel's masque, *The Vision of the Twelve Goddesses,* was presented at Hampton Court "by the Queenes most excellent Majesty, and her Ladies." The success of the *Pane-*

gyrike Congratulatorie and the continued efforts in court on his behalf by Lucy, Countess of Bedford, probably led to Daniel's being designated as the proper person to write the masque, which was a part of the festivities that were to enliven the first Christmas spent by James and Anne in England. The *Panegyrike,* delivered in the previous spring at Harrington Burleigh, which belonged to Lucy's father, may be regarded as the key to the favor of James which the poet gained so early. Among those taking part in the entertainment were Lady Penelope Rich (Sidney's "Stella") as Venus, the Countess of Hertford as Diana, the Lady Lucy herself as Vesta, and Queen Anne as Pallas. Dudley Carleton, who was present at the spectacle, wrote to his friend John Chamberlain: "Only Pallas had a trick by herself for her clothes were not so much below the knee, but that we might see a woman had both feete and legs which I never knew before." [15] We learn of a "Mr. Sanford," probably Daniel's old colleague at Wilton, who is to direct the "order and course of the ladies" in the various masks.[16] At the king's command, the wardrobe of Queen Elizabeth was rifled for the sumptuous occasion[17] that was to inaugurate a long procession of masques and shows in which the pleasure-loving Queen Anne delighted.

The occasion for Daniel's printing the masque is stated in his Preface "To the Right Honorable the Ladie, Countesse of Bedford": it was printed as a result of "the unmannerly presumption of an indiscreet Printer, who without warrant hath divulged the late shewe at Court." [18] Offended by this surreptitious edition, the poet published his authentic version giving a description of the entertainment. This event takes us back to a similar occasion in 1592 when Daniel first published his sonnets following the surreptitious edition of a "greedie Printer" Newman. It almost seems that Daniel profited by these piracies inflicted upon him; at least, he turned them to account. Further on in his Preface the services of Lucy in his behalf are acknowledged when he says that, by publishing the masque, he "might cleere the reckoning of any imputation that might be layd upon your judgement, for preferring such a one, to her *Majesty* in this imployment, as could give no reason for what was done." [19] This statement hints at the merit of his piece.

In literary quality the *Twelve Goddesses* is inferior to Daniel's subsequent *Tethys Festival,* and it lacks the poetry and dramatic effectiveness found in the later masques of Ben Jonson and John Fletcher. But the phrasing is occasionally lucid, and the versifications is smooth and melodious. For example, the final song, sung by the Three Graces, contains a rather subtle thought that is smoothly articulated:

> For comforts lock't up without sound,
> Are th'unborne children of the thought:
> Like unto Treasures never found
> That buried lowe are left forgott.

At one point the introduction of Iris, the many-colored messenger, to announce the approach of the goddesses Juno, Ceres, and others, looks ahead to the later masque in Shakespeare's *Tempest.*

One of the most interesting features of this masque is Daniel's explanation of how the goddesses will be introduced. In the Temple of Peace, Iris gives notice to the Sybilla of the approach of the goddesses and hands her a "Prospective, wherein she might behold the Figures of their Deities, and thereby describe them; to the end that at their descending, there might be no stay or hinderance of their Motion, which was to be carryed without any interruption, to the action of other entertainments that were to depend one of another, during the whole Shew: and that the eyes of the Spectators might not beguile their eares as in such cases it ever happens, whiles pompe and splendor of the sight takes up all the intention without regard [to] what is spoken; and therefore was it thought fit their descriptions should be delivered by the *Sybilla*." [20] And, in the spoken part of the masque, it so happens. The machinery of this masque is often awkwardly managed, and one writer has pointed out how particularly clumsy was this device of giving the sybil a telescope so that she might describe the goddesses before their entrance.[21] While it is true that Daniel's explanation may be intended to conceal his own lack of art, it also reveals his awareness of the important dramatic principle of "suspense of form." The poet here has described an art which Shakespeare learned and mastered well, but an art of which many playwrights still seem to be ignorant.

IV *Vicissitudes*

Shortly after this court entertainment Daniel was appointed licenser for the Children of the Queen's Revels. All plays proposed to be acted by the group had first to be submitted to him. On his appointment to the post, or shortly afterwards, he was made one of the grooms of the privy chamber to Queen Anne, for at this time the leading members of the various acting companies, including that of the Children of the Revels, were appointed to the honorary rank of Grooms of the Royal Chamber.[22] At any rate, the poet later so styled himself on the title page of *Certaine Small Workes* (1607).

If his *Philotas* was produced by the Revels Children in 1604, the displeasure it apparently incurred did not prevent Daniel's continuing to act as licenser for the boys' company.[23] It has been suggested that his connection with the company ceased when he permitted the Revels Children in 1605 to stage *Eastward Ho,* a play so offensive to the king that Queen Anne withdrew her patronage from the company. There is also evidence that Daniel as licenser had gone to considerable trouble to obtain a patent for Edward Kirkham and others to produce plays, performed by the Revels Children, at Blackfriars' Theater. In return for these services Kirkham and his associates became bound for a yearly payment to Daniel. Records show that the poet was forced to sell the bond on April 28, 1605, in order to meet other debts, and that he thus severed all connections with Kirkham and the others. The failure of Kirkham to continue payments on the annuity to the assignee led to a court suit that dragged on until 1609—one in which Daniel was called to testify.[24]

What this incident shows is that, despite his rapid access to royal favor, Daniel appears to have soon run into difficulties. Although he probably remained a groom of the royal chamber, very little assistance was coming from other quarters. These hints of pecuniary distress are no doubt related to his assertion in the 1605 letter to Devonshire that *Philotas* would not have been completed in 1604 had he not been overmastered by his necessities. The temporary withdrawal of Mountjoy's patronage at this time also seems likely.

In these years Daniel at times also reflects a spiritual isolation.

There is bitterness in some of the satirical scenes in *The Queenes Arcadia*, written in 1605, and the dedication of *Philotas* to Prince Henry, in which Daniel calls himself "the remnant of another time," is chill and sad throughout. The fact that most of this dedication, including the poet's hints that he has been excluded from royal favor, was omitted in the 1607 edition indicates that by this date his fortunes had perhaps once again improved. For the years from 1604 through 1606 he appears to have suffered a swift decline in his hopes; these were probably the darkest days of his career.

V *Sundry Poems and Other Pieces*

The *Philotas* made up part of a volume, *Certaine Small Poems*, which was composed of most of his earlier work, again revised, except for the *Civil Wars*. In the volume appeared for the first time one of the finest poems Daniel ever wrote, *Ulisses and the Syren*. Presented in the form of a debate between the claims of idle and sensuous beauty on the one hand and the life of heroic action on the other, it resembles in part Warwick's inner conflict that Daniel was to describe later in Book VIII of the *Civil Wars*.

The issues are not easily resolved in this poem, and it is questionable as to whether Ulysses or the Siren is the winner. The epistle to Southampton had stressed that true happiness comes with the arduous life, with trial by adversity. But in this poem the firm, virtuous, self-contained mind extolled in the *Epistles* is confronted with the subtler charm of luxury and of sensuality that is armed with a powerful sophistry. A wonderful modulation of the syllables and a mastery of assonance throughout the seventy-two lines slows the movement of the poem to the tempo of reasoned debate. This effect is shown in the Siren's opening speech, offering the traveler ease and freedom from toil:

> Come worthy Greeke, *Ulisses* come
> Possesse these shores with me:
> The windes and Seas are troublesome,
> And heere we may be free.
>   Here may we sit, and view their toile
> That travaile in the deepe,
> And joy the day in mirth the while,
> And spend the night in sleepe.[25]

Ulysses' answer is that the fame and honor of which he is in quest comes not with ease but with toil. Her reply is that his honor is empty, "begotten onely to molest/ Our peace." Real manliness, he replies, finds joy in toil. At this point in the poem Ulysses has partially accepted pleasure as a desirable end, and he has almost fallen into the trap when he says that the overcoming of difficulties is always recreated in the memory as pleasure. Her rejoinder is that there are many kinds of pleasure and that her sports do not bring on misery and bloodshed as his do. To which he replies that the state of things requires great-spirited men to overcome by war the evils of a "wicked peace." To all of which the Siren has the last word. The paradoxical nature of beauty is conveyed in her claim that she will be the eventual victor:

> Well, well *Ulisses* then I see,
> I shall not have thee heere,
> And therefore I will come to thee,
> And take my fortunes there.
> I must be wonne that cannot win,
> Yet lost were I not wonne:
> For beauty hath created bin,
> T'undoo, or be undonne.

There is also victory for Ulysses; he will not passively respond to pleasure but have it on his own terms.

One of the charms of this poem is that Daniel's characteristic indecision and his tendency to see both sides of a question operate in such a way as to leave the ethical problem open. The sensuous world, which is usually kept well in the background of Daniel's writings, here makes its claim, not so much by concrete and lush detail as by an elevated didacticism. The Siren "is no voluptuous Spenserian temptress, she is rather a disembodied attitude of mind, and her language is, so to speak, as manly as that of Ulysses." [26]

The poet A. E. Housman is loud in his praise of *Ulisses and the Syren,* but he adds that great poetry is capable of an emotional tinge which moves and touches, and in his view Daniel's poem does not achieve this effect. Yet Daniel has seemingly kept the emotion of this poem true to its subject, which aims beyond the personal to the universal. Of the first stanza Housman can hardly say enough in praise: "Indeed a promising young poetaster could not do better than lay up that stanza in his memory, not necessarily as a pattern to set before him, but as a touchstone to keep at his side. Diction and movement alike, it is perfect. It is made out of the most ordinary words, yet it is pure from the least alloy of prose; and however much nearer heaven the art of poetry may have mounted, it has never flown on a surer or a lighter wing." [27]

Himself a translator and close student of language, Daniel's continuing interest in it is shown by his dedicatory sonnet in 1605 to Joshua Sylvester's translation of Du Bartas' French epic, the *Divine Weeks,* and by the lines signed "S.D." in Peter Erondel's *French Garden* (1605). The latter poem of twenty-four lines has never been reprinted in any of the editions of Daniel, but it has been ascribed to him by such scholars as Harry Sellers, Joseph Ritson, F. G. Fleay, and W. C. Hazlitt.[28] Daniel was evidently a friend of Erondel, whose *French Garden* offers instruction in French pronunciation, grammar, and vocabulary, and then presents thirteen dialogues in French with English translation on a wide variety of topics pertinent to the time of day, occupations and businesses, and social and religious activities. It is a manual of language with some flavor of the courtesy book. Women play an important part in these dialogues. Since the printed commendatory poem is signed "S.D." and since it places much emphasis on the equality of women, one sees these factors as significantly related to Daniel's customary sympathy and respect for women.

Erondel had a well-known predecessor in the writing of language manuals. Claude Desainliens, whose English name was Claudius Holyband, was a French Huguenot schoolmaster who wrote a large number of manuals from the 1570's through the turn of the century. He was an older man than Erondel, who in later times (1619) revised one of his books. Several of Holyband's manuals were in conversational form, and one of these, his *Compo di fior, or else the flourie field of foure languages,* he dedicated in 1583 to Lucy Harington.[29] No doubt as a tutor Daniel had used the books of both men, particularly of Holyband; for he playfully chides Erondel in these lines for being so long in getting out his book but commends him for giving women a prominent part in it. The sober, dignified lines (41–42) in the epistle to Lucy should be set beside the jaunty, bouncing lines of the "S.D." poem:

> Ladies have long'd to match old *Holliband*
> That they with men might parle out their parte:
> Their wittes are rare, and they have tongues at hand,
> Of nature full, their onely want is Arte:
> Where former age regarded not their neede,
> Before all others thou hast done the deede.

These are recognizable attitudes of Daniel, and elsewhere in the poem are other signs of wit and humor.

Another work, doubtfully ascribed to Sir John Harington, may also have come from Daniel's pen. A prose treatise, *The Prayse of Private Life*, is with some additional matter largely a paraphrase of Petrarch's *De Vita Solitaria*. This work remained in manuscript form until recently when N. E. McClure included it in his edition of Harington.[30] Both Daniel and Harington, who was also a distant relative of Lucy Harington, were friends and may have occasionally met at Kelston, Harington's place in Somersetshire.

The treatise is composed of fifty short chapters comparing and contrasting the ways of life of the "busied man" and of the "solitarie man," but the latter is heavily favored. The "busied man" seems to have accumulated all the undesirable qualities—gluttony, lust, greed, sleeplessness, lack of content—as contrasted with characteristics of the solitary, contemplative man. However, without books and learning, solitude is seen as imprisonment and torture. The author condemns personal profit as a motive for academic education. The solitary life, it is finally conceded, is best fitted for learned man and lovers of virtue. The company of the few, and not of the many, is recommended. Much space is devoted to the desirability of fleeing from the city to the country: "Let us leave wise men in Townes, to tell money and use theire Arithmeticke." It seems better than an even chance that the treatise is Daniel's. The phrasing ("capable of truth") slightly suggests Daniel, and the subject seems more the kind that would interest him than it would the translator of *Orlando Furioso* and author of *The Metamorphosis of Ajax*.

Daniel probably had also a considerable hand in the London publication in 1606 of his brother John's book entitled *Songs for the Lute Viol and Voice*, never reprinted in entirety. In the six years since he had taken the degree in music at Oxford, John Daniel had probably become well established, with the aid of Egerton and others, as a notable musician. On the evidence of this one published copy of his music, he is said to rank high as a composer, and in some pieces to have carried, according to the *Oxford Companion for Music*, chromaticism far for his period. And for its discussion of the term "chromatic," Grove's *Dictionary of Music and Musicians* gives as an example Daniel's "Chromatic Tunes" from the 1606 volume. A recent publication, the *Historical Anthology of Music*, includes one of his songs with the words and the score from the 1606 *Songs*, and with this commentary, "Among the numerous English masters of the ayre John Danyel takes a prominent place, particularly because of his subtle feeling for textual declamation." [31] This textual quality of the *Songs* bears upon his poet-brother's collaboration. The volume contains fresh versions of two of Daniel's sonnets, "Like as the Lute delights" and "Tyme cruell tyme" set to music, and Daniel's bibliographer says that other songs in the book suggest by their style the poet's authorship.[32] There is considerable evidence to support this statement.

The dedicatory lines to "Mrs. Anne Grene/the worthy Daughter to/Sr. William Grene of Milton/Knight" are in alternate rhymes and much in the style of the poet-brother, though they are followed by John Danyel's name. The musician-author, having gracefully demonstrated the advantage of publishing to the world these songs that had been so intimately his and Anne Grene's (his pupil), still has some misgivings that are reflected in a passage that probably refers to his brother Samuel:

> Though I might have been warn'd by him, who is
> Both neare and deare to mee, that which we give
> Unto these times, we give t'unthankfulnesse,
> And so without unconstant censures, live.

It was in the period when Samuel was in a despondent mood.

One of the songs is very near to the poet in diction, in tone, and in the stoic mood reminiscent of the *Epistles:*

> He whose desires are still abroad I see,
> Hath never any peace at home the while:
> And therefore now come back my hart to mee,
> It is but for superfluous things we toile.

The remainder of this song and another one of three stanzas, beginning "Let not Chloris think because," strongly suggest Samuel Daniel's presence. Still another song in three stanzas, with its alternate rhymes, its sustained building metaphor, and its sobriety of tone, bears traces of the poet. It begins:

> If I could shut the gates against my thoughts,
> And keepe out sorrow from this roome with-in:
> Or memory could cancell all the notes,
> Of my misdeeds and I unthink my sinne,
> > How free, how cleare, how cleane my soul should lye,
> > Discharg'd of such a lothsome company.

The imagery of room and wall bearing the contrast between the inner and outer worlds is sustained throughout in this more than merely competent poem.

VI *Mountjoy and Daniel's Funeral Poem*

With the death in 1606 of his old friend and benefactor, Charles Blount, Lord Mountjoy and recently created Earl of Devonshire, Daniel must have arrived at one of the saddest, most solitary moments of his life. On this occasion he wrote a poem of some four hundred lines, part "character" and part elegy, which he revised and expanded a year later by adding epic elements. This much neglected work—one of the noblest in English heroic elegy and a poem once admired by Wordsworth, Coleridge, and Southey—still awaits the attention it justly deserves from modern readers. For it is a manly poem on one of the most admirable figures of his time, one in stature above Essex and closer to Ralegh, for Mountjoy possessed the qualities which could call forth Daniel's highest admiration. In low, measured tones, with emotion evident yet always in characteristic control, this poem is the fullest document of Daniel's affection and admiration for his chief patron, and it is also one of the largest portraits of a contemporary in Elizabethan literature. The subject of Daniel's elegy should first be looked at as he stands in history and in the estimate of his contemporaries.

Charles Blount, eighth Lord Mountjoy and Earl of Devonshire, was born in 1563. His great-grandfather had been a learned man and the friend of Erasmus. The scholar William Camden, after referring to this ancestor, speaks of Mountjoy in 1605 as "no lesse famous for his vertue and hereditary love of learning." [33] Blount did not complete his studies at either Oxford or the Inner Temple, and in 1583 made his way to court where the favor shown him by Queen Elizabeth aroused the jealousy of the impulsive Earl of Essex and led to a duel in which Essex was wounded. After their reconciliation, the two men remained friends until Essex' death in 1601. One of Mountjoy's early ambitions was to recover the wealth and reputation his family had been losing through a variety of excesses. [34] Perhaps for this reason he is reported to have been sparing in dress and frugal in habits. Fynes Moryson, later secretary to Mountjoy in Ireland, relates how the latter told him that "in his childhood when his Parents would have his picture, he chose to be drawne with a Trowell in his hand and this Mot: Ad reaedificandam antiquam Domum." [35]

He actively served his country as a member of parliament, as a commander in the Low Countries and in Navarre, and in various naval engagements. In 1594 he became Lord Mountjoy on the death of his brother, and shortly afterward he probably became Daniel's patron. Although he was busy in preparing the defenses of Portsmouth against Spanish attack, he managed in these years to devote much time to books and study and to the society of poets and men of learning. We know from the successive tributes paid to him by Daniel in the *Civil Wars* that the poet's attachment was a continuing one; and, despite the cloud cast over their friendship by the *Philotas* affair, close ties existed between them until the nobleman's death, as the *Funeral Poem* testifies:

> The benefite thou gav'st me to sustaine
> My humble life, I loose it by thy death:
> Nor was it such, as it could lay on me
> Any exaction of respect so strong,
> As to inforce m'observance, beyond thee,
> Or make my conscience differ from my tongue. [36] (25–30)

[*124*]

After Essex' failure to put down Tyrone's rebellion in Ireland, the queen named Mountjoy as his successor. Before this time he had become involved in the Essex conspiracy, and it is possible that he first undertook the Irish command with the intention of using his troops to support Scottish intervention in England. Although an accessory to the plot, he changed his mind later and refused to participate in the plans. Yet the queen, recognizing Mountjoy's talents in war, was willing to overlook his earlier implication in the plot; and Mountjoy himself knew that at court he was wholly at the mercy of his friend, Lord Secretary, Sir Robert Cecil.

The Irish campaign was long and costly, but Mountjoy's energy and persistence began at length to tell. By the summer of 1601, he had captured Tyrone's chief stronghold; and, on December 24, he gained a great victory over the Irish and Spanish forces at Kinsale. In the following year, he completed his conquest; but Queen Elizabeth died before her victorious commander returned to England in 1603 after three years of war to be created Earl of Devonshire and accorded many other honors by King James I.

Mountjoy's last years were clouded with a scandal that had its origin many years earlier. Before 1590 he began an intimacy with Penelope Rich, the sister of Essex and the wife of Lord Rich, with whom she had a most unhappy marriage. Penelope, Sidney's "Stella," bore Mountjoy five children before her divorce from Rich in 1605. In the same year, after prolonged effort, Mountjoy, now Devonshire, finally won ecclesiastical sanction to marry Penelope. Their marriage, which offended King James and Queen Anne and others at court, was of brief duration; for Devonshire died on April 3, 1606, after a short illness.

All the contemporary writers concur about Mountjoy's character; they see him as brave, conscientious, industrious, and as loyal to his friends. Daniel's praise of his deceased patron in the *Funeral Poem* is not so unqualified and exaggerated as Sidney Lee seems to think in his sketch of Mountjoy in the *Dictionary of National Biography*. A great deal of what the poet sees is in agreement with such contemporary observers as Robert Naunton and Moryson, whose accounts were not published until after Daniel's death; and we may suppose that some of the details in the poem that are not found in contemporary records proceed from direct observation by the poet whose view may have influenced these historians.

In Daniel's mind there was something of epic dimension in Mountjoy from the start. Indications of this regard are scattered through the *Civil Wars*. Three sonnets prefixed by Joshua Sylvester to his translation of Du Bartas' "Seconde Weeke" attest to the solid place Daniel had won in the affection of Mountjoy; and, in the third of these sonnets, written in 1598 or 1599, the latter is thus addressed with reference to the poet:

> Though Hee, thy *Homer* be; Thou, his Achilles;
> Both by each other Happy: Thou (here-in)
> T'have such a Trump as his immortal Quill-is;
> He such a Theam as thy High Vertues bin.

Daniel may be making a similar reference in the *Funeral Poem:*

> For there rests behind
> A Trophey to b'erected, that will stay
> To all posterities, and keepe in mind
> That glorious act which did a kingdome save,
> Kept the Crowne whole & made the peace we have.
> (270–74)

From these allusions comes the strong suggestion that Daniel either wrote or intended to write an epic celebrating Mountjoy's exploits. The nearest work we have to such an undertaking is the *Funeral Poem*, which may be regarded as Daniel's partial effort to make up for the deficiency. It is significant that nearly all the material added in the second (1607) edition is, as has been noted, epic in nature.

The *Funeral Poem* is written in alternate rhymes *abab*, Daniel's favorite arrangement, the monotony of which is relieved by couplets that occur at irregular intervals throughout the poem. His characteristic word-play is exemplified by "grace . . . disgrace" (9–10), and by "portes . . . important . . . transports" (227–29). Noticeable, too, is the frequency with which a key word in one line is carried into the next, as "will say . . . could say" (385–86).

Daniel's theme is introduced without delay in the slow, hushed opening lines of the poem:

> Now that the hand of death hath laid thee there
> Where neither greatnes, pomp, nor grace, we see
> Nor any differences of Earth and where
> No vaile is drawne, betwixt thy selfe and thee:
> Now *Devonshire* that thou art but a name
> And all the rest of thee besides is gone
> When men conceive thee not but by the fame
> Of what thy vertue and thy worth have done.

The inner qualities of Devonshire are effectively realized through the frequent employment of Daniel's favorite image, the building-metaphor. Thus, the promise of a sincere report comes early:

> How that brave minde was built and in what sorte
> All the contexture of thy heart hath beene,
> Which was so nobly fram'd, so well compos'd
> As vertue never had a fairer seate
> Nor could be better lodg'd nor more reposd,
> Then in that goodly frame, where all things sweet,
> And all things quiet, held a peacefull rest.   (35–41)

This well-built stoic mind is next seen as the most precious "furniture" possible for such a residence as Wanstead:

> And whereas many others have we see
> All things within their houses worth the sight,
> Except themselves that furniture of thee
> And of thy presence, gave the best delight.   (75–78)

There emerges the image of a strong, stable edifice which is at last fatally attacked by disease; but the moral qualities are unimpaired. In the closing lines the whole poem is seen as a "monument" and as a "trophey." In a world in which "the proudest frames that mans invention makes" are trampled upon and obliterated by time and nature, another tomb, "made by thy virtues in a safer roome," has been erected in the poem.

The relaxed movement and restrained tone are characteristic of

Daniel's best manner. The details are more particularized than is usual in his poetry, probably because of his personal knowledge of Mountjoy. Indeed, the topical nature of the poem may raise slight obstacles to the modern reader. In its first form the work constitutes a "character" with a few lines of elegy. The second edition adds epic matter, so that in its revised form the poem celebrates the character and exploits of the hero. There is very little of the traditional lament or dirge—and none of the elaborate artificial elegiac machinery that "stellifies" the hero. It is about as successful as an elegy can be in holding to sober, explicit facts that are still charged with the poet's emotion. The Earl of Devonshire emerges not only an admirable human being but a credible one as well.

But Daniel was aware too of his hero's imperfection; and, in characteristic fashion, his momentary enthusiasm for the whole of Devonshire's conduct, including his moral lapses, gives way to a stricter standard of rectitude. Thus the following lines of the first edition condoning Devonshire's sins are later dropped:

> So that whatever he hath done amisse,
> Was underneath a shape that was not knowne,
> As *Jupiter* did no unworthinesse,
> But was in other formes, not in his owne.

Again, by toning down "a passed error" to "an imperfection" (339), the poet obviates some of the difficulty in reconciling his moral judgment with Devonshire's conduct.

Daniel's final judgment of his great patron deserves to be quoted, and nowhere is sober manliness better shown than in the eloquence and dignity of the closing lines of the poem:

> And thus great Patrone of my muse have I
> Paid thee my vowes and fairely cleer'd th'accounts
> Which in my love I owe thy memory.
> And let me say that herein there amounts
> Something unto thy fortune, that thou hast
> This monument of thee, perhaps may last.
> Which doth not t'every mighty man befall,
> For loe how many when they die, die all.
> And this doth argue too, thy great desertes

> For honour never brought unworthinesse
> Further then to the grave and there it partes
> And leaves mens greatnes to forgetfulnes.
> And we do see that nettles, thistles, brakes
> (The poorest workes of nature) tread upon
> The proudest frames that mans invention makes,
> To hold his memory when he is gone.
> But *Devonshire* thou hast another Tombe
> Made by thy virtues in a safer roome.

The seventy lines beginning with line 199 were added in the second edition. They give a circumstantial narrative of Mountjoy's conduct of the Irish War and alter the structure of the poem as a whole. In the earlier version Daniel had attributed his omission of details of the Irish campaign to "time" and to his "present griefes." But, in the second edition, though apologizing for the inclusion of exploits that demand a more "spacious Mappe," he nevertheless gives details of this epic matter. There is drama in the account of the rigors of winter, the advice offered Mountjoy to give up the siege, the latter's speech to his men inciting them to action, his invocation to the Lord of Hosts, and his resultant victory. All these details enshrine Mountjoy as a national and Christian hero, and they add epic dimension to the faithful soldier of the earlier version.

Daniel's "character," one of the very best portraits of an Elizabethan contemporary, is in some ways the model for Wordsworth's "Character of the Happy Warrior" two centuries later. He also bears an obvious similarity to Shakespeare's Henry V; his nocturnal vigil and his heroic speech at Kinsale are particularly close to Henry's conduct on the eve of Agincourt. Daniel's portrait may indeed derive from Shakespeare's. The idealized happy warrior in Shakespeare, Daniel, and Wordsworth is an interesting circumstance of literary history that is perhaps more than accidental.

By 1607 Daniel had passed through six years of changing fortunes and new associations. The later years had been rather unhappy ones after the promising start at the beginning of the century. Living on in a new reign and having lost his best patron, the Earl of Devonshire, he felt himself in 1607 as a remnant of another time. Meanwhile, he was striking out in new literary directions too.

CHAPTER 7

Another Kind of Drama (1604-1614)

IN THE decade following 1603 Daniel wrote two masques for court performance, *The Vision of the Twelve Goddesses* (1604) and *Tethys Festival* (1610), as well as two pastoral dramas, *The Queenes Arcadia* (1605) and *Hymen's Triumph* (1614). His *Twelve Goddesses* inaugurated the vogue of the masque upon which King James and Queen Anne lavished much attention and expense. Daniel was also an innovator in introducing the Italian pastoral drama into England. Assuming that he had met Battista Guarini in Italy around 1590 and knowing that Daniel was pleased with the first English translation of the *Pastor Fido* in 1602, we wonder why he had waited so long before imitating the Italian poet. The lag has been attributed to the rather conservative taste of the court circle in the closing years of Elizabeth's reign.[1] Probably a combination of factors—the poet's renewed interest in pastoral drama as a result of the recent translation, his new position at court, and the royal fondness for lavish pomp and entertainment—led him to write *The Queenes Arcadia*.

I *Pastoral Drama:* The Queenes Arcadia

Printed in 1606, the play, designated on its title page as *A Pastorall Trage-comedie*, was "presented to her majestie and her Ladies by the Universitie of Oxford in Christs Church, in August last. 1605." So it was apparently written early in 1605. Largely an adaptation of Guarini's *Pastor Fido*, Daniel's was the first play to exhibit on the English stage the direct influence of Italian pastoral drama. As part of the entertainment for the king and queen, it was one of four plays performed. John Chamberlain, the inveterate letter writer and gossip of the day, found the other three Oxford plays, all in Latin, tedious; "but the day of departure an English pastorall of Samuell Daniells (presented before the Queene) made amends for all, being indeed very excellent, and some parts exactly acted." [2] It is interesting to compare this favorable view of a play that posterity has regarded generally as imitative and dull with Chamberlain's dislike for Daniel's second pastoral, *Hymen's Triumph*, staged nine years later, a play usually adjudged greatly superior to the earlier work. In a letter of February 3, 1614, to his friend Dudley Carleton, Chamberlain anticipates the pastoral "that shalbe represented in a little square paved court" to entertain the king at the marriage of Lord Roxborough and Mistress Drummond. But, after having seen the performance, Chamberlain reports that "the pastorall made by Sa: Daniell was solemne and dull, but perhaps better to be read than presented." [3]

The title *The Queenes Arcadia* is reminiscent of the title of Sidney's romance, and it tells us that Daniel has written an "Arcadia" for the queen's pleasure. However, Daniel's conventional pastoral story has harsh, satirical overtones. Meliboeus and Ergastus, ancient Arcadians, lament over the way mistrust, disloyalty, deceit, and general corruption have been invading and destroying their country. Concealed, they observe young couples—exhibiting such usual behavior in lovers as jealousy, disdain, and unrequited love—being victimized by the scandal-peddling Colax, "a corrupted traveller," and by Techne, a subtle wench of Corinth. All comes out right for the shepherds in the end, and the culprits are rounded up and driven off.

Another pair of rogues, Alcon, a quack doctor, and Lincus, a pettifogger, try to upset the peace of Arcadia by suggesting the presence of diseases that don't exist, by peddling medicines with exotic names to the simple inhabitants, and by stirring up litigation among peace-loving people. This satirical element no doubt attracted the interest of a court audience at a time when the quack and the sharp-practicing lawyer were stock characters in contemporary satire and when considerable amusement was found in exposing the abuses of tobacco.

The plot very closely resembles its Italian sources,[4] and the events at times have little dramatic interest—especially the denouement that is mechanically contrived by having the two old Arcadians come forth from their concealment and expose the machinations of the scoundrels. The play, although generally dull, is enlivened by Alcon and Lincus, the comic characters as well as the butts of satire. The list of strange chemicals and medicines they peddle carries a contemporaneous note seldom found in Daniel, but one reminiscent of Ben Jonson. As in Jonson, the taking of tobacco affords opportunity for amusing comment. Says Alcon, who is corrupting people with this vile weed:

> For whereas heretofore they wonted were,
> At all their meetings, and their festivalls,
> To passe the time in telling witty tales,
> In questions, riddles, and in purposes,
> Now doe they nothing else, but sit and sucke,
> And spit, and slaver, all the time they sit,
> That I goe by, and laugh unto my selfe.

There is humor in this scene, but Daniel mars it later by intruding his own sober moralizing into the speech of this unscrupulous quack:

> But sure the time's to come when they looke backe
> On this, will wonder with themselves to thinke
> That men of sense could ever be so mad,
> To sucke so grosse a vapour, that consumes
> Their spirits, spends nature, dries up memorie,
> Corrupts the blood, and is a vanitie.[5]

The style in this play is often too formal and stilted, even when accompanied by graceful verse. This mixed quality may be perceived in the account of Cloris' behavior as she stands over her supposedly dead lover Amyntas:

> For we perceiv'd how *Love* and *Modestie*
> With sev'rall Ensignes strove within her cheekes
> Which should be Lord that day, and charged hard
> Upon each other, with their fresh supplies
> Of different colours, that still came, and went,
> And much disturb'd her.   (2108–13)

Whatever circumstances led Daniel to write the *Queenes Arcadia,* the theme of his story, much of it ready-made for him, was

congenial to his interest and tastes. He had extolled the simple life
in his earlier writings. He had protested against the endless complications in the doctrines of religious sects in *Musophilus* and
against legal equivocations and subtleties elsewhere, especially
in the epistle to Egerton. And once more he wants Arcadian simplicity preserved from all those forces—here dramatically presented as evil—which threaten it. There is a familiar Daniel ring
in the reprehensible Lincus' boast:

> And I can cite the law t'oppugne the law,
> And make the glosse to overthrow the text;
> I can alledge and vouch authority,
> T'imbroyle th'intent, and sense of equity.   (2527–30)

Another consideration that might have attracted him to pastoral
drama is that it is remote enough from history to be free from any
suspicion of contemporary political allusion. He had suffered
enough from the reception of his historical play that touched, in-
tentionally or unintentionally, on some sensitive spots in current
political life. In his dedication to the queen he takes great pains to
explain to her why he hasn't written such a play in this case, for
"in the view of state t'have show'd/A counterfeit of state, had
beene to light/A candle to the Sunne." And after this somewhat
weak explanation, he says that, since his "humble argument" was
born on the ground, he will erect there his scene, and safely too:
"And if we fall, we fall but on the earth,/From whence we pluckt
the flowers that here we bring." It is hard to avoid seeing the
cautious, once-bitten Daniel in these lines.

The *Queenes Arcadia* may have some connections with Shakespeare too. It has been said that the Oxford performance of the
play was possibly witnessed by Shakespeare and Daniel's work
may have suggested some of the imagery in *Macbeth,* first produced about a year later. Some three or four passages in the two
plays offer interesting parallels in imagery. In addition, several
unusual turns of phrase in Daniel's play are reminiscent of *Hamlet,* which was produced five years before it.[6] All these instances,
together with the signs in the "Cleopatra" plays of mutual influence between the two poets, suggest that they were familiar

enough with each other's writings to sometimes echo each other's phrasing and imagery.

II *The Second Masque:* Tethys Festival

Tethys Festival: or the Queenes Wake, was "celebrated" at Whitehall on June 5, 1610, and published later in that year. The title page states that it was "devised by Samuel Daniel, one of the groomes of her Majesties Honourable privie Chamber." This statement makes it clear that the poet still remained in the service of the queen. There was a double occasion for the celebration: the creation of Prince Henry as Prince of Wales and the ceremonies of the Knights of Bath. The masque that followed on these important festivities was presented by the queen and her ladies, and it was designed by Inigo Jones as an elaborate and expensive spectacle. The queen herself took the part of Tethys, and among the attendants as "the nymph of Ayr" was the Countess of Dorset, Daniel's old pupil Anne Clifford.

Tethys, Queen of the Ocean, receives tribute from her thirteen English river nymphs. Gifts are brought in from the tributaries and Tethys to the Ocean King. From Daniel's description, we may guess at the elaborateness of the appointments. One of the several scenes was a port or haven "and the figure of a Castle commanding a fortified towne: within this Port were many ships . . . seeming to be at anchor." The sea seemed to move with a gentle gale, with many sails passing in and out. The Tritons wore fins of silver from waist to knee and a mantle of sea-green laced and fringed with gold. Another of the scenes showed "severall caverns gloriously adorned." The queen's throne had as "basement" two whales of silver, the arm rests were "two cherubines of gold," and over her head was a scallop of silver. And there was of course much more.[7] The embroidering of the queen's dress alone cost fifty-six pounds, and upon the costumes of the fourteen ladies in the masque were lavished 10,920 yards of cloth at a cost of almost eleven hundred pounds.[8] All this lavishness, however, does not make the masque a great one.

Yet it is far more colorful and more dramatic than the *Twelve Goddesses.* It excels also in a lyric verse that is light and graceful. For example, the opening lines of the Tritons' song are well-suited to the occasion:

> Youth of the Spring, milde *Zephirus* blow faire
>   And breathe the joyfull ayre,
> Which Tethys wishes may attend this day;
>   Who comes her selfe to pay
>   The vowes her heart presents,
>   To these faire complements.   (92–97)

Another song, justly admired by Charles Lamb, who printed it in his *Dramatic Specimens* in 1808, has some of the airy, yet serious quality of certain of Shakespeare's songs:

> Are they shadowes that we see?
> And can shadowes pleasure give?
> Pleasures onely shadowes bee
> Cast by bodies we conceive,
>   And are made the thinges we deeme,
>   In those figures which they seeme.
> But these pleasures vanish fast,
> Which by shadowes are exprest:
>   Pleasures are not, if they last,
>   In their passing is their best.
>   Glory is most bright and gay
>   In a flash, and so away.
> Feede apace then greedy eyes
> On the wonder you behold.
>   Take it sodaine as it flies
>   Though you take it not to hold:
>   When your eyes have done their part,
>   Thought must length it in the hart.   (341–58)

In simplicity and vigor the final line is perfect.

Still another song of twelve voices, accompanied by the music of twelve lutes, as the nymphs proceed with flowers from the caverns, is lovely poetry. Its fine modulation of line length and its control of assonance remind us of the beautiful music that opens Spenser's April eclogue in the *Shepherd's Calendar:* "Ye dayntye Nymphs, that in this blessed Brooke." A considerable measure of that Spenserian music lives on in Daniel's poem:

> Was ever howre brought more delight
>   To mortall sight,

> Then this, wherein faire *Tethys* daignes to shew
> Her, and her Nymphes arow
> In glory bright?
> See how they bring their flowers,
> From out their watry bowers,
> To decke *Apollos* Tree,
> The tree of victory.
> About whose verdant bowes,
> They Sacrifice their vowes,
> And with an everlasting spring
> Of glory, to the Ocean King.   (306–18)

It is too often the mistake of critics and biographers to erect a framework into which a writer's achievement is neatly fitted by "periods," kinds of influences at work, phases of growth and decline. For Daniel, no such pattern can be discerned, nor ought it be forced. We know that, as the years went by, he tended to give up metaphor for abstraction, occasional audacity for discreet caution, vigor and color for sober fact. But the tendency was, after all, only partial. He seems to rally and return from time to time to the tender lyricism of his earliest verse. We find this in *Ulisses and the Syren* and in the plays and masques of his later years.

Both of Daniel's masques are inferior to those of Ben Jonson, and there is evidence of rivalry, perhaps hostility, between the two poets. No doubt the choice of Daniel to write the first queen's masque in 1603, because of the influence of the Countess of Bedford, aroused jealousies; for about the same time Jonson's verse epistle (*The Forest*, XII), in speaking of his devotion to the countess, probably refers to Daniel: "Though she have a better verser got,/ (Or poet, in the court-account), than I/ And who doth me, though I not him envy."

And now in 1610, following the decline in popularity of Jonson's masques, superior as they were as poetry, his rival was again chosen to write the queen's masque. Inigo Jones, the great stage architect, favored the grandiose and spectacular in his designs, which tended to encroach on the poetry that for Jonson was the paramount thing. For Jonson, the masque was a dramatization, an embodiment of poetry; for Jones, the poetry was more an embellishment of his splendid stage designs.[9]

Probably Daniel was more readily agreeable to Jones's ideas. His preface to *Tethys Festival* has been seen as a veiled attack on Jonson and as suggesting that Daniel is taking sides with the architect:

And shall we who are the poore Inginers for shadowes, & frame onely images of no result, thinke to oppresse the rough censures of those, who notwithstanding all our labour will like according to their taste, or seeke to avoid them by flying to an army of authors, as idle as our selves? . . . And for these figures of mine, if they come not drawn in all proportions to the life of antiquity (from whose tyrannie, I see no reason why we may not emancipate our inventions, and be as free as they, to use our owne images) yet I know them such as were proper to the business. (Grosart, III.306,307)

Daniel may be making an allusion to Jonson's adherence to sound poetic idea, backed up by literary and historical documentation. But we recognize too Daniel's earlier insistence in the *Defence* that we need not always build by the square of Greece and Italy.

III   Hymen's Triumph

Greatly superior to the *Queenes Arcadia* in every way is *Hymen's Triumph*. From its 1615 title page, designating it as a pastoral tragicomedy, we learn that it was presented "at the Queenes Court in the Strand at/her Majesties magnificent entertainement of the/Kings most excellent Majestie, being at/the Nuptials of the Lord/Roxborough./By Samuel Daniel." The marriage was between Robert Ker, first Earl of Roxburgh and a trusted favorite of King James, and Jean, daughter of Patrick Lord Drummond, on February 3, 1613/4 (in early 1614). For the marriage ceremonies, held in Somerset House, Queen Anne bore the cost of three thousand pounds. The Lord Mayor and the aldermen were invited the day after the wedding, and rich presents were exchanged.[10] Accompanying a manuscript copy of the play, now in the library of Edinburgh University,[11] is a fourteen-line verse dedication to the bride in Daniel's own hand, acknowledging with gratitude her honesty and kindness.[12] The dedication was replaced by one to the queen in the first printed edition of 1615.

From the poet's lines to Queen Anne it is apparent that he has continued to enjoy the royal support which by this time has become more munificent. He refers to the wedding festivities in Somerset House the year before, of which his play was a part:

> As being a piece of that solemnity,
> Which your Magnificence did celebrate
> In hallowing of those roofes (you rear'd of late)
> With fires and chearefull hospitality;
> Whereby, and by your splendent Worthines,
> Your name shall longer live then shall your walls.   (10–15)

This play also uses the conventional matter of pastoral drama, but W. W. Greg, who is sharply critical of Daniel as poet and dramatist, recognizes *Hymen's Triumph* and its Prologue as an original composition and as a departure from its Italian sources.[13] The opening Prologue (lacking in the manuscript) is appropriately delivered by Hymen, who in disguise is resolved to bring about the happy union of the Arcadian lovers, and by his archenemies Avarice, Envy, and Jealousy, who announce they will oppose and obstruct him. They too will be disguised and, like Hymen, do not appear in the play proper. This withdrawal of the personages who set the theme of the drama going is reminiscent of Shakespeare's device in the Induction to *The Taming of the Shrew*.

The action of the play moves towards Silvia's removal of her disguise as the boy Clarindo and her reunion with her lover Thirsis. As in some of Shakespeare's romantic comedies, a series of cumulative intimations about identity and vague reminiscences prepare the way for a final recognition that is not too sudden and jolting. One of these is Thirsis' wanting always to look at Clarindo, who he feels resembles his lost Silvia. Another occurs when old Medorus, father to the "dead" Silvia, has a dream in which she returns to gain his consent for marriage with her lover.

But the familiar and conventional entanglements of plot in pastoral drama—the separation, the capture by pirates miraculously converted to good, and the contrived reunion—may betray a dramatist into sentimentality and bathos, as is the case in this play. When Clarindo tells Thirsis her tale of the Arcadian boy (really herself) aboard the pirate ship asking mercy of the barbarous captain, his wife, and their son, and of these captors finally giving way in stereotyped order to uncontrolled weeping, the artificial qualities inherent in pastoral drama come to the fore. And then she continues her story of the "boy's" returning to Arcadia, while Thirsis, notwithstanding all his previous intimations of Clarindo's identity, is unable to make any connection at all and does not recognize her until later when he discovers a mole and feels her breasts after she has been stabbed by the jealous Montanus. A familiar enough development follows when the despairing Thirsis, believing her dead, attempts suicide. However, all comes out right when the lovers are restored by the medicinal arts of Lamia.

Hymen's Triumph bears a good many traces of some of the earlier romantic comedies of Shakespeare. Silvia's disguise as a boy, and, even more, her courage and her sweet womanhood, recall Viola in *Twelfth Night*. The similarity is especially notable in lines 241–53 of Daniel's play in which Cloris speaks of the resemblance between Silvia and her boy "Clarindo," and in the passage beginning with line 327, where Silvia broods over the false report that her Thirsis is in love with another. Furthermore, Daniel's presentation of the impatient, questioning lover is very much like Shakespeare's in *As You Like It*. Rosalind impetuously asks of Celia: "What did he when thou saw'st him? What said he? How look'd he? Wherein went he? What makes he here? Did he ask for me? Where remains he? How parted he with thee? And when shalt thou see him again? Answer me in one word" (III.ii.232–37). Daniel's Cloris similarly asks news of her lover:

> Tell me the manner where, and how thou foundst
> My *Thirsis*, what he said, how look'd how far'd,
> How he receiv'd my message, used thee:
> And all in briefe, but yet be sure tell all.   (824–27)

One final resemblance occurs when Thirsis, having found on the shore Silvia's torn veil and her lock of rent hair, guesses that she must have been devoured by wild beasts. We recognize a likely variation of the much-employed tale of Pyramus and Thisbe which appears also in *A Midsummer Night's Dream*.

In this last of Daniel's plays a variety of mood and a rich lyricism are to be found. The poet catches, for instance, some of the

Elizabethan half-playful, half-serious mood toward paradoxical love in the dainty song of the chorus concluding Act I "Love is a sicknesse full of woes," with its refrain, "More we enjoy it, more it dies/If not enjoyed, it sighing cries,/Hey ho." And, at the close of Act III a festive wedding song expresses a warmth and earthiness fit for the occasion:

> From the temple to the borde,
> From the borde unto the bed;
> We conduct your maydenhead:
> Wishing Hymen to afford
> All the pleasures that he can,
> Twixt a woman & a man.   (1338–43)

If there were a little more of this nearness to the physical world in Daniel's poetry, he might have occupied a somewhat more popular place in later esteem.

More of a piece with the whole body of his poetry is the serious, pensive mood that pervades the pastoral setting in this play. It is sober, but not severe; at times, it is tender. Daniel is the spokesman here, as ever, of the dignity of womanhood; and he recognizes in woman a spiritual guide to men. When Palaemon tries to dissuade Thirsis from pining away for love of a "silly" woman, Thirsis replies:

> And for a woman, which you prize so low,
> Like men that doe forget whence they are men;
> Know her to be th'especiall creature, made
> By the Creator as the complement
> Of this great Architect the world; to hold
> The same together, which would otherwise
> Fall all asunder; and is natures chiefe
> Vicegerent upon earth, supplies her state.   (1268–75)

That is the principle of cohesion and order which women serve, But Thirsis presses on to a vision of the true nature of woman's beauty:

> Thinke not it was those colours white and red
> Laid but on flesh, that could affect me so.

[140]

> But something else, which thought holds under locke
> And hath no key of words to open it.
> They are the smallest peeces of the minde
> That passe the narrow organ of the voyce.
> The great remaine behinde in that vast orbe
> Of th'apprehension, and are never borne.   (1283–90)

The conventional pastoral scene has here become immensely en-larged, for love is envisioned as part of the cosmic plan.

The poet also shows a power to invoke the sensuous world. There is a tender hushed beauty about the disguised Silvia's words to the sleeping Thirsis:

> sleepe thy fill, sweet love,
> Let nothing trouble thee; be calme oh windes,
> Lest you should wake my love: thou gentle banke
> That thus are blest to beare so deare a weight,
> Be soft unto those dainty lymmes of his:
> Plie tender grasse, and render sweet refresh
> Unto his weary senses, whilst he rests.   (1420–27)

In these lines all the images express quiet and repose; they have likewise a concentration of sensuousness. Perhaps no single piece of Daniel's expresses more variety of mood and feeling than *Hymen's Triumph*. That may be why, despite patches of mawkish-ness, it has called forth generous praise from its readers. It is a fitting close to Daniel's career as a dramatist. He had in a sense led the way in three aspects of English drama: French Senecan closet tragedy, the masque, and Italian pastoral. Although not spectacular, his achievement was distinctive and sometimes of high quality.

CHAPTER 8

The Prose History *and Last Days*
(1608-1619)

THE decade following the accession of King James I (1603–1613) was a busy and varied one for Daniel. In addition to the masques and plays, he wrote the *Funeral Poem,* numerous short pieces, and the prose *History,* his last major work. Moreover, in the collected editions of 1607 and of 1609 he made extensive revisions of such earlier work as *Cleopatra* and the *Civil Wars.* His Preface "To the Reader" in the 1607 edition of *Certain Small Workes* is the fullest expression of his credo as a practicing man of letters who, never satisfied with what he has done, "puls downe, and alters what he did the last/As if the thing in doing were more deere/Then being done & nothing likes thats past." Men of his stamp "ever make the latter day the scholler of the former. . . . As if there were no saboath of the minde." So he is led on to examine his defects all the more since, as he matures in sensitivity, he is increasingly aware of how elusive truth and perfection are:

> For man is a tree
> That hath his fruite late ripe, and it is long
> Before he comes t'his taste, there doth belong
> So much t'experience, and so infinite
> The faces of things are, as hardly we
> Discerne which lookes the likest unto right.[1]

Nothing better illustrates the caution, diffidence, and honest uncertainty of Daniel than these lines.

I *The Last Active Years*

Thomas Fuller says of Daniel in these years that "he would lie hid in his garden-house in *Old Street,* nigh London, for some months together (the more retiredly to enjoy the company of the Muses) and then would appear in public to converse with his

friends, whereof Doctor Cowel and Mr. Camden were principal"
(500). The reference here is to William Camden, the antiquary,
and John Cowel, professor at Cambridge. Camden's popular *Remaines* in 1605 has fine things to say of "our Lucan," quotes a
passage from the *Civil Wars,* and proceeds to assign Daniel high
rank. After offering in this commonplace book quotations from
writers of former times, Camden remarks, "If I would come to our
time, what a world could I present to you out of Sir Philipp Sidney, Ed. Spencer, Samuel Daniel, Hugh Holland, Ben Johnson,
Tho. Campion, Mich. Drayton, George Chapman, John Marston,
William Shakespeare, & other most pregnant witts of these our
times, whom succeeding ages may justly admire" (6,8).

The garden house referred to by Fuller was likely that of Simon
Waterson, old friend and publisher for both the poet and Camden. Gerald Langbaine, writing a half-century after Fuller, adds
the detail that, as a consequence of Queen Anne's generosity, the
poet was enabled "to rent a Garden-House near London, where in
private he composed most of his Dramatick Pieces." [2] It is not
clear whether Fuller had these same years in mind when he wrote
that in his old age Daniel "turn'd *Husbandman,* and rented a
Farm in *Wiltshire.*" Evidently Daniel spent long periods of time
in both city and country in this last decade of his life; his fine
prefatory tribute to his "deare friend and brother," John Florio, in
the latter's *Queen Anne's New World of Words* in 1611 concludes
with the phrase "Thus from my plow."

Residence in the country must have begun as early as 1607,
judging from the evidence afforded by two letters from Daniel
addressed to Pye Corner in Hertfordshire to James Kirton, an officer in the Earl of Hertford's household. [3] In the first of these,
dated May 20, 1608, the poet calls Kirton "Charissimo patron'
mio" and refers to himself as a poor bailiff. Such details as the
price of hay and the wranglings among tenants keep him busy. He
does not seem to be very happy in administering the details of the
farm since he expresses distaste for his present occupation: "Thus
I ame fayne to descend in my particulars, that in my generall
acount do somme & cast up the busynesses of princes and convers
dayly in my quiet with the best of the earth." About this time he
was revising and expanding the *Civil Wars,* and he was living at
the Garden House when he could find time from his duties as

bailiff in the country. The letter makes clear that the Earl of Hertford, who had discussed the subject of "the Passion of a Distressed Man" with Daniel several years before, has given assistance to the poet, who, one may judge, was forced by economic necessity to accept a way of life not altogether to his taste. The largess from the queen was evidently insufficient.

The second letter, written from town a few days later and dated May 31, 1608, reveals that Daniel has hastened thither at the request of his "Lord," presumably the Earl of Hertford, and is apparently waiting orders. He tells Kirton that, while in London, he is living at the Garden House, and that he is unwilling to come to Canon Row, where the Earl of Hertford resides,[4] for "to be often seene in the Cittie . . . of some I would not see, might much prejudice mee." Having made two journeys to the Temple, he has not been able to met Kirton's brother Josias, who, we know, was also in the employment of the Earl of Hertford and is recorded as being approved for the post of Muster Master of Wiltshire,[5] where the farm was located at which Daniel was said to have "turn'd Husbandman." James Kirton himself is listed twice among the commissioners engaged in surveying lands for the Earl of Hertford, and he is said to be "of the Middle Temple." [6] The wording of the rest of the letter suggests that Hertford, the Kirton brothers, and Daniel were involved in an important project in which the poet was proud of his own role as mediator and conciliator.

How long he remained on the farm we do not know. Enough evidence from the sheer mass of his activities—revision of old work and the beginning of new—assures us that he must also have been in the city and at court for the performance of a masque in 1610 and again for a pastoral drama in 1614. Before the publication of his prose *History* in 1612, he probably spent considerable time in London, say from 1608 to 1611, in gathering and reading additional sources for that learned work. This seems to be the case because, in his later prose dedication of *The Collection of the Historie of England* to Queen Anne, Daniel says that the history appertains of right to the queen, "being for the most part done under your roofe, during my attendance upon your sacred Person." [7] The conversations with Camden may well have taken place in those years.

In dedicating his 1609 edition of the *Civil Wars,* Daniel returns to his early patroness, the Countess of Pembroke. With this edition, which brings the history only two-thirds of the way through to its projected end in the Tudor peace, all work on the poem ceased; the poet was now proposing to write a history in prose. In his dedication to the countess he refers to the kind of writing he had done in the *Civil Wars:* "For mine owne part, I am not so far in love with this forme of Writing (nor have I sworne Fealtie onely to Ryme) but that I may serve in any other state of Invention, with what weapon of utterance I will. . . . And because I finde the common tongue of the world is Prose; I purpose in that kinde to write the Historie of England, from the Conquest: being incouraged thereunto by many noble & worthy Spirits." [8] He was probably already embarked on his new venture.

II *The Prose* History

Daniel's chief work in prose began as *The First Part of the Historie of England,* published in 1612 and reissued in 1613. It was preceded by a lengthy epistle "to the Right Honourable Sir Robert Carr, Viscount Rochester," which was replaced by another addressed to Queen Anne in the much expanded edition of 1618, titled *The Collection of the Historie of England.* In the original dedication Daniel outlines the scope of his book. It will consist of three sections, the first of which contains three books: (1) England to the coming of the Norman; (2) the reign of William I; (3) William II through Stephen. "And this part I have done," he writes (IV. 76). This section therefore constitutes *The First Part of the Historie of England.* The second section was to begin with Henry II and extend through the Wars of the Roses, but Daniel got only as far as Edward III—where his *Collection* ends. The third section, which he never began, was to extend from the first Tudor to his own time. He proceeds in his dedication to sketch some of the great advances made in more recent history, where so much has been attained with so little bloodshed. Finally, he promises Carr that the king may be assured that the author "will tread as tenderly on the graves of his magnificent Progenitors, as possibly I can: Knowing there may (in a kind) be *Laesa Majestas,* even against dead Princes" (IV.78). In his "Certaine Advertisements to the Reader" in the later 1618 edition of the *Collection* he apologizes on the ground of ill-health for not progressing faster with his task (IV.81). Another reason offered is his striving for perfection in all he attempts: "I had rather be maister of a small peece handsomely contrived, then of vaste roomes ill proportioned and unfurnished." Then follows his citation of authorities for the various sections of the *Collection*. He promises to be fair and to report honestly in accordance with integrity, "the chiefest duty of a Writer" (IV.83).

Daniel's list of sources includes William of Malmesbury, Roger Hovedon, Giraldus Cambrensis, Matthew Paris, Nicholas Trivet, John Caxton, Jean Froissart, Thomas Walsingham, Polydore Virgil, Robert Fabian, Richard Grafton, Edward Hall, Raphael Holinshed, John Stow, John Speed. These and many other historians he drew upon as his work developed and enlarged. The *Collection* (hereinafter called the *History*) reveals still more extensive reading. His skeptical attitude towards fables was already evident in *Musophilus;* in his *History*, he turns it to account in the critical management of some of his more credulous sources.[9] In general he employs his sources judiciously, using one for the structure of a particular period, like that of Edward II, and another to fill in the details of such an outline. He moves from one to the other insofar as each account contributes to a coherent, factually reliable understanding of the whole; he abandons, therefore, what he thinks is an unreliable account for one more trustworthy.[10]

A close and intensive study has been made by Rudolf Gottfried of Daniel's use of one very important source, the anonymous *L' Histoire et Cronique de Normandie*, published in 1578 and in several later editions. The poet might have read it on his first visit abroad, where, as he tells Carr in the dedication to his *History*, he first "especially took these notions." Gottfried presents numerous passages showing parallelism in substance and language between the two writers. The evidence is adjudged "extensive and minute," but Daniel does not merely copy. He condenses, combines, expands. He abbreviates a source well and succeeds in changing its tone. He makes inferences implying historical causation, and he adds reflections of his own. Gottfried concludes that the *History*, unlike the larger compilations of Holinshed and Stow, "was an attempt to reinforce the claims of truth with those of literary art." [11]

It seems probable that *A Breviary of the History of England,* not printed until 1693, and doubtfully ascribed to Sir Walter Ralegh, is likewise the work of Daniel. Careful comparison of matter and style of the *Breviary* with the *First Part* and the *History* indicates that it was a first short sketch by Daniel, out of which the longer versions grew.[12] Since the manuscript of the *Breviary* was addressed to the Earl of Salisbury, Robert Cecil, who held this title from 1605 until his death in 1612, Gottfried concludes it must have been written within that space of time. Moreover, Daniel had made a proffer of service to Salisbury, then Lord Cranborne, in his apologetic letter of 1605 regarding *Philotas*. This bid for favor may have led to his addressing the *Breviary*, first draft of the *History*, to Cecil.[13]

The *History* reveals characteristic moods and attitudes of Daniel: a love of England; a sense of fairness and justice regardless of class; a balanced judgment in seeing that all times and peoples have their merit. He is not merely chronicling events; the moral judgments on men's actions are there, written as old proverbs or as his own *sententia*. First we recognize one of his old peeves, the Norman subtleties of the English law. Discussing the common law in the reign of William the Conqueror, Daniel recognizes that the Norman Code was more universal and equitable than the variety of English laws it replaced. Yet he strongly disapproves of laws in a foreign tongue, whether in French or in Latin. He shows how English finally reasserted itself over French-Norman after the Conquest in all areas except the law. And his revulsion against the old "Norman subtleties" emerges again when he says, "nor have we now other marke of our subjection and invassalage from *Normandie*, but onely that, and that still speakes *French* to us in England" (IV.167). He prefers again the directness, plainness, and simplicity of English to the subtleties of the litigious Norman. His allegiance to his native tongue should not be mistaken for insular ignorance, for Daniel was accomplished in foreign languages. But, like many great humanists before him (for example, Sir John Cheke) Daniel sponsored the free development of his own language and its liberation from foreign linguistic bondage.

A good example of Daniel's balanced judgment, of his awareness that there is a character to each historical epoch—and this was rare for his time—occurs after he has cited the Conqueror's praiseworthy traits of character. Then he adds, "But these may be as well vertues of the Time, as of Men, and so the age must have part of this commendation" (IV.182). Another passage shows sharp moral insight, incisive, witty commentary, neatly wrapped up in a characteristically sententious conclusion. Both King Richard I and the French king are rivals, though now in league in the Holy Land. The French king wishes to return to France, no doubt to do mischief to England in Richard's absence. The reluctant Richard finally agrees to the solicitation of his rival, who leaves. And so Richard "writes invective letters against the King of *France*, for leaving him. Who likewise defames King *Richard* amongst his neighbors at home. And it may be doubted whether the perjury of these two kings did not adde more to their sinne, then the action they undertooke for the remission thereof could take away, for that *A good worke impiously managed, merits no more than an ill*" (V.10).

Daniel sees in the reign of Henry III, as elsewhere in his *History*, some of the folly and lack of judgment displayed in the crusades, as well as the practical and political purposes behind them. His most unflattering account of all English kings is that of John, monster and traitor, who displays these mixed qualities of stupidity and cunning. Fairness is shown in his account of Henry III, in whose reign Daniel sees the causes for the long drawn-out First Barons' War as proceeding from faults on both sides (V.141). For Henry's reign had "many examples of a crasie and diseased State, bred both by the inequality of the Princes manners, and the impatience of a stubborne Nobility" (V.141). Daniel, as noted earlier, is ever on the side of patience and against turmoil and violence, perhaps a state of mind that limited him emotionally as an epic poet. He tended to see, as a true historian, both sides of an issue, a quality better suited perhaps for the *History* than for the *Civil Wars*.

This balanced political judgment and this moral reflection become more assertive in his account of the reigns of Edward I and his successors. The brave and equally foolhardy Edward is shown at the time he was proclaimed King of England in Palestine and later when he accepted a challenge on his return to England to a tournament by the Earl of Chalbourn, "wherein again hee hazards his person to shew his valour, which may seeme to be more then became his Estate, and Dignity" (V.142). Edward is drawn as an able, energetic king whom Daniel in the main admires and applauds for endeavoring, in the long war with the Scots, to bring the whole island under one government. Daniel is ever for peace, but he insists that it must be attained on equitable grounds. Hence he adds, "Yet all such actions hath much of iniquity, so had this, and wee see it was not force or the Sword could effect it. . . . Violence may joyne Territories, but never Affections together; which onely must grow voluntary, and be the worke of it selfe" (V.155). After this observation, Daniel characteristically pays tribute to the brave Scots in a war which he deeply regrets should have had to take place at all—a war which in reality accomplished so little.

There is increasing generalization and moral commentary as the *History* moves on through the reign of Edward I. After telling how the king gained concessions from several of his political opponents, the author adds: "But it is not well with a State, where the Prince and the people seeke but to obtayne their severall ends, and worke upon the advantages of each others necessities: for as it is un-sincere, so it is often unsuccessfull, and the good so done hurts more, then it pleasures" (V.162). Of Edward's illness and death during an invasion of Scotland, we are told that he died "at *Borough* upon the Sands, as if to shew on what foundation he had built all his glorie in this world" (V.175). This swift summation of a whole career recalls the terse, grim couplet in the *Civil Wars* which concludes the account of the beheading of Suffolk at Dover: "Part of his blood hath *Neptune,* part the Sand;/As who had mischiefe wrought by sea and land" (V.101).

Daniel's treatment of the reign of Edward II shows balance and understanding of the diverse qualities in men. It opens with mention of how the young king's riotousness, disorder, neglect of state, and advancement of favorites were disastrous to his people and to the office of king. And though some of these excesses might be excused as a "first sicknesse" of his youth, "those often Relapses of his shewed it was an habitual indisposition in the whole state of his minde, not to be cured" (V.177). When Edward is defeated by Bruce at Bannockburn, Daniel is scrupulously fair about advantages and superiority. It is true, he says, that the Scots were greatly outnumbered, but it is also true that they were more hardened to battle than the English and had the advantage in position. Both halves of this statement produce a neutral balancing and afford comfort to the claims of both sides. Forced by parliament to resign his crown in favor of his son, the deposed King Edward was imprisoned and later murdered at Berkeley Castle. In his account of these events, the author, despite his low estimate of Edward II as king, is deeply sympathetic toward him in his sufferings.

Edward III is greatly admired; he is "most renowned for valor and goodness . . . a mighty king, glorious and triumphant." One of his first acts, which must have helped endear him to Daniel, was—on petition of the Commons—to require that all pleas be made in English, not French. The historian comments: "a blessed Act and worthy so great a King, who if he could thereby have rendered the same also perspicuous, it had bene a worke of eternall honour, but such is the Fate of Law, that in what language soever it speakes, it never speakes playne, but is wrapt up in such difficulties and mysteries (as all professions of profit are) as it gives more affliction to the People then it doth reamedy" (V.268–69). Now, while the old contempt for the Norman subtleties again presents itself, the whole statement is made with wry humor. The wretched law, as it were, is fated to be obscure, even in English; then a partial explanation is found in its being linked with baser occupations. And the *mystique* of finance is nicely caught too.

Great as was this king, the beam is seen as turning after his first forty years of rule. And, when Daniel brings his *History* to a close, he sees a design of justice operating in English history, as he looks ahead to the reign of Richard II: "His stepping over his Fathers head to come to his throne, though it were not his fault, yet had it a punishment and that in most high kinde." For, though Edward had seven sons, not one of these but a mere child succeeded him; and he was exposed to a factious state and to ambitious uncles. All the conquest that is left to Edward III at his death is Calais. And the *History* concludes with the statement that all this is "to show that our Bounds are prescribed us; a Pillar set by Him who beares up the Heavens, which we are not to transpasse" (V.290).

Ill-health or discouragement prevented Daniel from completing the prose history, as we see from a final note: "And heere I leave, unlesse by this which is done, I finde incouragement to goe on" (V.291). But the design of the unfinished work is clear. He had brought the prose history to the point were the *Civil Wars* began, and he would have enlarged the role of Nemesis as an ever return-ing justice, placing it at the center of the action; but he would probably have divested Nemesis of its metaphorical gear. The causes of the Wars of the Roses, we see from this concluding par-agraph of the *History*, are pushed back in time from Bolingbroke's usurpation and beyond Richard II's immaturity to Edward III who, through no design of his own, came to the throne as succes-sor to a weak though outraged king. Daniel's conclusion adum-brates the theme of usurpation that runs through the Wars of the Roses and suggests that Daniel's conception of English history was widening as he progressed. There is also the possibility that, as he approached the period of the *Civil Wars*, he was faced with the problem of writing anew on what he had done well in the earlier poem. The difficulties ahead might have offered a discour-aging prospect to a man who was already ill and was to die within a year from the time his *History* was published.

III   *Last Honors, Failing Health, and Death*

In these last years, as ill-health came upon him, the poet seems to have prospered materially. Accompanying the publication of his *History* in 1618 came a royal grant, dated March 11, of special privilege and authority to Daniel, "one of the Groomes of the Queenes Majesties most Honorable Privy Chamber," for the print-ing of the book. Three years earlier, in 1615, he had been granted by the Office of Revels permission to manage a company of youths to perform comedies and tragedies at Bristol. In June, 1618, the office passed into the hands of his brother John.[14] As groom in the queen's household, along with Florio, Daniel received an annual wage in 1616 of sixty pounds.[15] Both he and Florio marched in the queen's funeral procession in 1619, as they had marched together seven years earlier at the death of young Prince Henry.[16]

His brother's succeeding him to the Revels post in June, 1618, was no doubt occasioned by the poet's failing health. There are indications of this decline in his verse letter, written in June, 1618, to James Montague, the ailing Bishop of Winchester.[17] Montague died of jaundice and dropsy the next month, on July 20. The lines describing the bishop's illness as slow in its attack and as free from sudden, frightening surprises—an illness from which the writer too suffers and which enables him the more readily to sympathize with Montague—clearly indicate jaundice as the fatal disease:

> And though it show us dayly in our glasse,
> Our fading leafe turn'd to a yellow hue,
> And how it withers as the sappe doth passe,
> And what we may expect is to ensue. (55–58)

This poem is the last one we know of from Daniel. It is in the same spirit as that of the earlier epistles and of the dedications to Bodley and Montaigne. The poet offers the ailing but spiritually well-fortified bishop additional ammunition—the consolation that this disease comes slowly and kills subtly, thereby allowing him time for study and thought. The poet knows, "For that my selfe have struggled with it too,/And know the worst of all that it can do" (13–14). The final consolation to the dying man is the assurance of his having done so much to restore and rebuild the great cathedrals of Daniel's native region, particularly at Wells:

> And so long as the Walls of Piety
> Stand, so long shall stand the memory of you;
> And Bath, and Wells, and Winchester shall show
> Their faire repaires to all Posterity. (67–70)

But even more important is the fact that Montague has built not only walls but worthier edifices—men. And this last of Daniel's poems fittingly ends with a characteristically sententious couplet: "For when can men go better to their rest/Then when they are esteem'd and loved best?"

During the next year the queen too passed away. Daniel had some time before this event retired to a farm called "The Ridge" near Beckington in Somersetshire. He made his will on September 4, 1619, saying that he was "sick in body but well in mynd," and he requested that his body be interred in the church of the parish where he died. His "faythfull Brother John Danyel" is named sole executor; and, as overseers of his will, he names a "brother-in-law John Phillipps" and his faithful old publisher-friend, Simon Waterson. He names no wife or direct descendants in this will, a portion of which is in his own "rather tremulous hand." [18]

A month later, on October 14, the poet died at Beckington. Long afterward, the Lady Anne, Countess Dowager of Pembroke and Dorset erected a memorial to him—a plain monument on the inside of the north wall of the church. The inscription reads:

> Here lyes, expecting the second comming of
> Our Lord and Saviour Jesus Christ, ye Dead Body
> of Samuel Danyell, Esq., that Excellent Poett and
> Historian, who was Tutor to the Lady Anne
> of Clifford in her youth, she that was sole Daughter
> and Heire to George Clifford Earl of Cumberland
> Who in Gratitude to him erected this Monument
> in his Memory a long time after when she
> was Countess Dowager of Pembroke, Dorsett
> & Montgomery. He dyed in October 1619.

Daniel, a modest and retiring man, possessed an enduring dedication to literature and to the conviction that he had a place in it. Upright in his relations with people and free of vulgarity, he might have seemed overfastidious to some of his more robust contemporaries; it is, therefore, not an accident that Jonson felt antagonism to him. Daniel was fundamentally conservative, urging moderation wherever compatible with principle. His retiring nature, however, did not stand in the way of his winning favor with the great; it was likely a social advantage. He must have hated scenes and fuss, for he avoided the brawling marketplace and sought the quiet refuge and protection of patrons, despite its dangers of sterility.

His sense of having lived on into another, less friendly age appears more than once in his later writings. Yet he seems to have prospered just as much in Jacobean as in Elizabethan times. The sense of death was growing stronger, and it is fitting that his last poem was about death and the moral resources which man can muster to face it. He, who was so persistent an editor and reviser, would have been pleased to see the posthumous edition of all his poetry which his brother John brought out in 1623. It has a pleasant association in time with another and much greater posthumous edition, Shakespeare's First Folio.

CHAPTER 9

Poet and Thinker

ANY reassessment of Daniel as a poet should take note of what his own contemporaries found in him. The early poet of the sonnets, *Rosamond, Cleopatra,* and the first five books of the *Civil Wars,* won more ready acceptance than the later author of *Musophilus,* the *Epistles,* and the *Funeral Poem on Devonshire.* Writing in 1614 or earlier, epigrammatist Thomas Freeman, plays with the Latin motto frequently appearing before Daniel's published works, *Aetas prima canat veneres postrema tumultus,* and provides in somewhat awkward verses an index of the poet's popularity in both phases of his career:

> I see not (*Daniel*) why thou shouldst disdaine,
> If I vouchsafe thy name among my mirth;
> Thy *aetas prima* was a merry vaine,
> Though later Muse tumultuous in her birth:
> Know, here I praise thee as thou wast in youth;
> Venerous, not mutinous as now;
> Thy Infancie I love, admire thy growth,
> And wonder to what excellence twill grow,
> > When thou shalt end the broils thou hast begun,
> > Which none shall do, if thou shalt leave undone.[1]

Other contemporaries express this somewhat mixed appraisal, ranging from praise to censure, and indicate an uncertainty about Daniel's merit as a poet. Nashe and Barnfield, among others, eulogized him. William Browne called him "well-languaged Daniel," and William Drummond of Hawthornden thought he was "for sweetness in rhyming second to none." On the other hand, Spenser, while recognizing Daniel's gifts, admonished him to rouse the feathers of his low-flying muse; and Drayton, at first under the influence of "the sweet Musaeus of these times," later found him to be "too much historian in verse." Ben Jonson's harsh judgment that Daniel was no poet was partly balanced by Edmund Bolton's comment that "the works of Samuel Daniel contained somewhat a flat but yet withal a very pure and copious English, and words as warrantable as any man's, and fitter perhaps for Prose than for measure." [2]

Later writers are cautious too about his poetic achievement, though with a difference. They show a preference for his work of the middle period—*Musophilus,* the *Epistles,* and in general the *Civil Wars.* In the eighteenth century, Thomas Gray thought that Daniel's style rarely rises to elevation, that "his figures and allusions are neither many nor bold," but that *Musophilus* reveals a genuine talent for elegy.[3] Coleridge shortly afterward found still more to praise: Daniel's "diction bears no mark of time" and "is pre-eminently pure—of that quality which I believe has always existed somewhere in society." But Coleridge also saw much that is prosaic; and admirably reconciling Daniel's limitations with his merits, Coleridge found in his work "that style, which as the *neutral ground* of prose and verse, is common to both." [4]

Subsequent critics have said much the same thing: Daniel's note is pitched low, his style is sober and chastened, he lacks redhearted passion. W. MacNeile Dixon has suggested that Daniel's grace and eloquence and his measured deliberate style adumbrate the early eighteenth century, "the age of prose and reason," and that he was an exponent of the Classical style in English and one of its founders, a forerunner of the Augustans, a correct poet before Pope.[5]

The consensus then has been that Daniel was "well-languaged," though at times flat and prosy; that he had a grace and smoothness; but that he lacked vigor and daring. There seems never to have been much doubt about his gravity and his competence as a sound historian. Closer examination of his diction, his versification and imagery, and his pervasive sense of history should provide larger ground for appraisal.

I *Diction and Rhetoric*

Daniel's vocabulary is deceptively simple in the sense that so many of his words are of later common acceptance. Few colloquialisms are to be found in his writings, and the language of contemporary occupations or amusements is rare. There are few references to the specific aspects of rural and urban life—of the London shop or of the English countryside. Even his portraits of individuals have very little particularity, for it is their moral nature, rather than their physical qualities or outward manners, that he dwells upon. This characteristic is but another aspect of his predilection for the general and the abstract—a quality that would have no doubt proved a serious obstacle to his success as a writer for the popular stage.

A tendency to generalization is shown in Daniel's growing fondness for a less vivid Latinate diction—as an examination of his numerous revisions indicates. Whether he was aiming to make up for a poor rhyme or to correct a metrical irregularity, the changes are predominately Latinate. A few examples from the 1609 revision of the *Civil Wars* alone are "labour" for "work," "lamentable" for "wofull deadly," "current" for "maine," "subvert" for "overthrow," "considering" for "seeing," "desp'rate" for "headlong," "conducting" for "leading." Such alteration may result in a loss of directness and vividness, but it sometimes arrives at greater precision or smooths the rhythm. So, in the change from "Conclude some hope of quiet, to take breath" to "Gave some calm leisure to recover breath," we see how deftly a procession of harsh consonants is eliminated and assonance is improved. Again, we find "Began to grow to be of fearefull might" smoothed out beautifully to "They grew to be of formidable might." The poet breaks up a string of monosyllables in "A base meane man whom few or none would miss" and writes "A base companion, few, or none, would misse."

Another aspect of Latinate diction is Daniel's predilection—evident in all stages of his career—for words prefixed by *en* and *in;* these prefixes are generally used to intensify the original verbal or substantive idea. Some of the words of this kind which he introduced are now obsolete or rare: "imbetter," "in-common," "instarre," "intenerat," "invile," "invulgar'd." Others originating with him that have remained are "infolded" (relating to arms), "embroylement," and "innovate" (intransitive). In the *Panegyrike Congratulatorie* he refers to Henry VII as "there great *Exemplare, Prototype* of Kings" in a line providing the earliest instance in our language of these two words from Latin and Greek.

Daniel is not a practitioner of the pun, a fact which might help to explain his "purity" and modernity to us. Since the pun exploits words on several levels of meaning from "received standard" to contemporary slang and vulgarism, it quickly loses much of its meaning. When he does pun, he is almost always within the more recognizable limits of standard "book" usage. A few examples from the *Civil Wars* make this point clear:

> *Aumarle* became the man, that all did marre.   (III.49)[6]
> . . . .
> Attended with his fatall fier-brand
> Of Warre, *Warwicke*.   (VII.5)
> . . . .
> Anjou and Maine (the maime that foule appears)
> Th'eternall scarre of our dismembred Land).   (VI.16)[7]

Usually, Daniel is content with even more transparent word-play in such passages as "The under-takers have been over-tooke" (III.11) and "Yet happy-hapless day, blest ill-lost breath" (VI.99). He likes the oxymoron in such phrases as "faire-fierce," "feeble-force," "happy-hapless," and "gently-severe." One of the more lavish displays of it occurs in Caesarion's speech: "Then wretched greatnesse, proud rich misery,/Pompous distresse, glittering calamity" (*Cleop.*, 1001–2).

A related form of word-play that pervades his writing is paranomasia, the variations in meaning of a word or root-word through successive phrasings. Three examples will suffice:

> Worke what she could, she could not worke to stay.
>   (*Cleop.*, 1428)
> . . . .
> For most of all the rest, toyld in unrest.
>   (*Civil Wars* [1594], I.9)
> . . . .
> For now the Spaniard hath possesst three portes
> The most important of this Ile say they
> And sooner fresh supplyments, *Spaine* transports.
>   (*Fun. Poem*, 243–45)

There are also intricate inversions—fraught with meaning—like the concluding lines of the final chorus from *Cleopatra*: "Doth

Order order so/Disorders overthrow?" Daniel manages the word-play in such a manner that it scarcely seems a contrivance, a trick of style, but a necessary outgrowth of the context to give balance and weight to his statement.

A large part of his alleged prosiness no doubt comes from a sometimes tiresome, almost never ending succession of connective devices. At least that is the impression made particularly by *A Letter to Octavia*. When Coleridge condemned stanzas seven, eight, and nine of the first book of the *Civil Wars* as illustrative of "the prosaic Daniel" and "solely because the words and their order would find appropriate place in prose, and are not suitable to metrical composition," he must have had this objectionable quality in mind.[8] In Daniel's later work particularly, there is a growing incidence of such introductory devices as "whose," "which," "where," "since," "as if," often with a vague or abstract antecedent. And the result is a kind of loosely floating stanza, one not sufficiently moored down by concrete substantives.

These defects are apparent in the otherwise admirable *Musophilus*. At several points in this poem a succession of stanzas introduced by these feeble connectives—in one instance "and" is used to introduce each of four consecutive stanzas—saps the vital movement of the whole. The lack of strong particularized verbs and nouns causes the stanza to languish. Without these, or an occasional epithet or exclamation, the attention keeps slipping away. The long, involved passages, with simple enough diction, become so smoothly spun from their almost hidden antecedent bases that it is often hard to find a passage of three or four lines that will stand by themselves. Not the line, nor the stanza, but the paragraph as we understand it in its prose sense is operating here. We may see this characteristic in the following lines in which the poet describes the "greater wittes" who fail to attain the success they expect and must witness the good fortune of inferior persons:

> They present with the sharpe of *Envie* straine
> To wound them with reproches and despight:
> And for these cannot have as well as they,
> They scorne their faith should daigne to looke that way.
>   (*Mus.*, 462–65)

Another colorless use of a pronominal connective is the rhyme formula, "the same." A distinguishing mark of Daniel's style, it occurs more often in his works than in those of any other of his contemporaries, except possibly Fulke Greville.[9] Occurring at all stages of Daniel's writing career, it usually does no more than add a faded, colorless effect to the line which it ends. It becomes a ready-made resource for rounding out a rhyme with "flame," "shame," and "fame." Perhaps the employment almost exclusively throughout his verse of alternate rhymes tempted Daniel to fall back upon this stock phrase. Of the many examples from his work, the most appalling is probably "This is the last: if we discharge the same,/The same shall last to our eternall fame" (*Civil Wars*, VI.81). No doubt this is another aspect of style that earned the epithet "prosaic Daniel."

He was a most careful and painstaking reviser, even though some of his tinkering occasionally marred a better early effort. He liked to work over certain phrases, indeed whole lines, in subsequent poems.[10] These close parallels in phrasing are likely to appear between works being composed and those being revised around the same date, and they tell us something about the poet's economical use of materials. If he found an attractive phrase, he might put it to further use. Thus the 1592 sonnet begins "Let others sing of Knights and Palladines" (*Delia*, XLVI). In revising the sonnets in 1594, while at the same time writing the *Civil Wars*, he reworked the line into another context: "Why do you seeke for fained *Palladines*/(Out of the smoke of idle vanitie)" (V.4). From *Rosamond* in 1592, the line "Now drawes the date of mine affliction neere" (429), becomes in the *Civil Wars*, "Or was the date of thine affliction out" (V.41). The phrase "capable of truth" appears in one of the 1603 epistles (*To the Lord Henry Howard*, 65–66) and again in the 1605 *Philotas* (411–12). Sometimes, after a long absence, an old familiar line turns up once more. Thus the "sweet silent rethorique of perswading eyes" in 1592 (*Rosamond*, 21) reappears in 1605 as "Ah 'tis the silent rhetoricke of a looke" (*Queenes Arcadia*, 2159–60).

One of the most interesting examples of this reworking of phraseology occurs in at least four different contexts. The 1594 dedication to *Cleopatra* contained the line, "And makes of all our honours but a pray" (45). In the following year there appear in the *Civil Wars* the lines, "Doth this great All, this *Universall,* weigh/The vaine designes that weaknesse doth begin?" (I.117) When *Cleopatra* was revised in 1599 the two passages were made to coalesce: "That else in darknesse carries all away,/And makes of all an universall pray." Appearing in the same volume with this revised *Cleopatra* was the new poem *Musophilus,* into an early section of which the phrasing of the 1595 *Civil Wars* is introduced. Here we read "That all this little All, might not descend/Into the darke a universall pray" (37–38)—somehow related also to the revised *Cleopatra* passage. Further on in *Musophilus* comes the now familiar phrasing: "To make of all a universall pray" (246). From such examples we may see something of the poet's modes of composition.

II *Versification*

Daniel wrote sonnets of the "Shakespearian" form; narrative poems in rime royal and six-line stanza, rhyming *ababcc;* an epic narrative poem in ottava rima; epistles of varying stanzaic form, including terza rima; and choral songs of varying rhyme. They all have one thing in common—alternate rhyme. He concedes that tragedy "would indeede best comporte with a blank verse," except for the choruses; but his own practice even in tragedy was to use the alternate rhymes predominately. Yet he was sensitive to the monotony of regularly recurring rhymes, and he therefore tried especially in his later work for variety *within* the pattern most dear to him. What he did to vary this "over-glutting the ear" through alternate rhymes is related in his *Defence of Ryme:* "I have assaid in some of my Epistles to alter the usuall place of meeting, and to sette it further off by one Verse, to trie how I could disuse my owne eare and to ease it of this continuall burthen . . . but as yet I cannot come to please myselfe, therein: this alternate or crosse Ryme holding still the best place in my affection" (156).

And he holds to this rhyme consistently with the variations he speaks of. The concluding couplet of both the ottava rima and the rime royal stanzas are only variations of the prevailing alternate rhyme, which is dominant also in the terza rima of the epistle to Lucy, as it is in the one to Lady Margaret in which he delays "the place of meeting" by one verse. With *Musophilus* the case is somewhat different. In it the stanzas are often so closely interlocked that they almost lose their identity as a structural unit. One long section of the poem especially (737–880) consists of six-line stanzas in alternate rhyme that are so interlinked that the fifth line of one stanza anticipates the first line in the next, producing a rhyme pattern that might be represented as *ab ab cb/cd ed/ef ef gf/gh gh ih*, and so on. The anticipating rhyme carries an effect of light surprise, for it is unrelated to the alternate rhymes immediately surrounding it, and it carries the reader's attention forward, past the final line, into the stanza beyond. What happens is that the rhyme sounds are diminished or muted, and the discourse is continuous, with the tonal effect of prose.

It is not only that alternate rhymes are delayed or varied in Daniel's stanza. In most of his later verse he frequently aims at inexact or approximate rhyme. Examples are "contriving it—contradict," "tell—laudable." Sometimes identical syllables or unaccented sounds produce a faint rhyme, like "ominous—frivolous—Hippopotamus" and "mysteries—subtleties—sympathize." These sounds are not so far different from the feminine and *ion* rhymes which the poet sought to eliminate when revising his earlier work. Whatever their limitations in other verse, they seem to be particularly suitable to the reasoned discourse and the meditative tone of such poems as *Musophilus*, the *Epistles*, and large portions of the *Civil Wars*. As a consequence, rhetorical display is subordinated to the quiet play of thought. Coleridge found the effect most pleasing: ". . . the interspersion, I mean (in stanza poems) of rhymes from polysyllables—such as Eminence, Obedience, Reverence? To my ear they convey not only a relief from variety, but a *sweetness* as of repose—and the Understanding they gratify by reconciling Verse with the whole wide extent of good Sense." [11]

Coleridge also likes, as I think most readers do, Daniel's frequent grace in adapting the movement of thoughtful conversation to narrative verse by slowing the latter down through emphatic use of polysyllables. And Coleridge's fine ear for metrical subtleties is evident from his scansion of Daniel's line: Hŏw lōng hăve Ī lōngd tŏ bĕhōld thăt fāce.[12]

Yet Daniel's accent was faulty, and he knew it. In his Preface to the 1607 *Certaine Small Workes,* he twice apologizes for bad accent and attempts to justify his revisions on the ground that he works toward ideal meaning and clarity. He is certain that he will be read "among the rest/So long as men speake english," but he is also cognizant of the ever changing fashions of authority in language. His self-doubt is shown in the line, "For though I hold not accent I hold sence"; and he returns to it later in the poem: "And would to God that nothing falty were/But only that poore accent in my verse."

Daniel perhaps draws more attention to his limitations by his meticulous revisions. He apparently wanted to get away from the somewhat sugary, early verse; and he trimmed his poetry down to leaner lines, even working toward a harsher, more irregular meter as he strove for a vigor that he never fully attained. This effort is shown in his occasional bold management of elisions. Contrary to general practice, he not infrequently forced normally accented words into positions where they elided—and with very harsh effects. We see this in such apocopations as "shalb' addrest," "n'occasion," "b'unhappy," "h'indures," "b'example." Though some metrical regularity is retained in these cases, there is considerable loss in euphony. Sometimes the consonant sounds are so compressed that a line becomes very difficult to pronounce, as in the epistle *To Henry Wriothesley:* "God sets to act the hards't and constant'st parts" (60). Yet, considering the theme of that poem— the nobility of courage set against adversity—the rugged line seems appropriate. What is lacking as poetry in many of these cases is variety of metaphor.

III *Metaphor and Abstraction*

Daniel's revisions and later new work show a gradual loss in concreteness of imagery and a marked increase in abstract phrasing that draws very close at times to the prosaic. This drift is less easy to detect in such early works as the *Delia* sonnets and *Rosamond* because in them the acquired imagery of the sonnet tradition going back to Petrarch is a sustaining element. There are reminiscences of the sonnet metaphors in *Rosamond,* as in the stanza beginning "Thou must not thinke thy flowre can alwayes florish" (239), which contains several of the metaphors of sonnet forty-two that begins "Beautie, sweet love, is like the morning dewe."

And such a passage as "Com'd was the night, mother of sleepe and feare,/Who with her sable mantle friendly covers" (432–33), has behind it the imagery of the famous forty-fifth sonnet, "Care-charmer sleepe, sonne of the sable night." And, when the abstractions do occur in *Rosamond,* they generally emerge with a sustained vigor. We take, for instance, this stanza:

> The mightie who can with such sinnes dispence,
> In steede of shame doe honors great bestow:
> A worthie author doth redeeme th'offence,
> And makes the scarelet sinne as white as snow.
> The Majestie that doth descend so low,
> Is not defilde, but pure remaines therein:
> And being sacred, sanctifies the sin.   (288–94)

Each line has at least one verb, forceful enough to render the passage vivid, despite the abstractions. Another passage is equally effective:

> Treason was in my bones my selfe conspyring,
> To sell my selfe to lust, my soule to sinne:
> Pure-blushing shame was even in retiring,
> Leaving the sacred hold it glory'd in.
> Honor lay prostrate for my flesh to win.   (309–13)

Each line presents an image, consisting of an abstraction supported by a concrete element. The effect, here and elsewhere, is attained with relatively little sensuous imagery, perhaps through the poet's ability to shift quickly and smoothly from concrete object to abstract idea. The attention is not allowed to rest long on the object; the actual seeing is withdrawn and the mind is now allowed to work upon the relationships between the abstractions, with occasional return to the concrete.

This happy fusion of abstract and concrete is found abundantly in Daniel's poetry, as these further examples will show:

Confusion onely rowles, Order sits hie.   (*To the Lady Anne,* 55)

Sweet silent rethorique of perswading eyes.   (*Ros.,* 121)

If rage spar'd not the walls of pietie,
Shal the profanest piles of sinne keepe strong? (*Mus.*, 121–22)

. . . .

Written in ice of melting vanitie. (*Mus.*, 130)

. . . .

And never man had heart more truly servd
Under the regiment of his owne care. (*Fun. Poem*, 83–84)

. . . .

Base malediction, living in the darke,
That at the raies of goodnesse still doth barke.
(*To the Lady Margaret*, 90–91)

The impression that Daniel lacks metaphorical variety possibly
comes from the fact that his metaphors elude our awareness because they are so closely linked with the abstractions. Hotspur's
rousing speech (*Civil Wars*, III.101), beginning with "This day
(saith he) ô faithfull valiaunt frendes," has very little apparent
metaphor; but the abstractions seem to move along under their
own power. This could be said also of the lines on Talbot (VI.93),
in which the half-emerged metaphor of a wrestling match is built
upon such unpromising abstract materials as "ardor" and "years."
All these passages may well be what Henry Wells meant by the
"Sunken Image"—one that occurs where metaphor is observed
and no definite picture is called to mind although it powerfully
affects the imagination.[13] According to Wells, both Shakespeare
and Daniel are rich in the vocabulary of this hinted metaphor.

By 1599 Daniel's tendency toward abstractions becomes greatly
accelerated. Fewer metaphors are present; in fact, there are so
few that they are often dissolved by the abstractions. A good example of this dilution of the concrete by abstractions and obscure
connectives is found in *Musophilus:*

> For emulation, that proud nurse of wit,
>   Skorning to stay below or come behind,
>   Labors upon that narrow top to sit
>   Of sole perfection in the highest kind;
>   Envie and wonder looking after it,
>   Thrust likewise on the selfe same blisse to find:
> And so long striving till they can no more,
>   Do stuffe the place or others hopes shut out,
>   Who doubting to overtake those gone before

Give up their care, and cast no more about;
And so in skorne leave al as fore-possest,
And will be none where they may not be best.   (259–70)

Despite the fact that *Musophilus* is a fine reflective poem, with rich veins of elegy and impassioned prophecy, there are moments when it seems overlong, tedious, and dull. There are stretches where practically all sensuousness has been abandoned, and we find ourselves listening to a weighty argument, almost in the approved manner of a Fulke Greville treatise. At these points, the attention slips away, for we can *see* nothing.

The epistle to Sir Thomas Egerton is another poem marred by a dimness of metaphor, which on some occasions comes to life. The abstractions operate almost as allegory: Injunction stays the hand of Altercation; Equity renders judgments worthy the respect of Peace and Amity; Wrong enters at the very gate designed for Right and is masked in a coat of Law, which in turn sets a trap to catch Ignorance and entangle Intemperance. All this abstraction had been better suited to prose, where the needless allegorical disguise might be dropped for direct and literal statement of fact. Instead of establishing the correspondence between the image and its abstract meaning and then letting the metaphor do its work, Daniel keeps shuttling back and forth between image and idea through a whole complicated sequence of actions. The consequence is that the reader cannot hold the two structures simultaneously since the metaphorical one has not been established. For example, at the beginning of this poem, Egerton is compared to an isthmus dividing the two oceans of Rigor and Uncertainty—an appropriate figure—but this vivid analogy fades in the next three lines when the currents of wrong and pride enter to confound the supporting images as well as the idea.

Much of the poet's imagery then is muted or submerged. The considerable body of images that do emerge are easily sensed and classified by most readers. Daniel is not rich in variety of colors: there are of course, red, green, blue, and the others; but whiteness and transparency predominate; and "clear" is one of his favorite words, employed in a wide variety of senses. There are a number of metaphors of fire, particularly in the *Civil Wars*. But what predominates is the concentration upon the objects of movement, smoothness, and repose. The largest and most obvious forms for conveying these qualities are the water-figures that are abundant particularly in the earlier poetry and the building-figures that are progressively dominant from 1599 on. These are not mere chance creations of a single line of verse; they are usually extended similes and metaphors that in some cases (the *Funeral Poem,* for instance) enter into the total thought and design of the poem.

In *Shakespeare's Imagery* Caroline Spurgeon discusses the many river metaphors, saying that this marked interest is quite peculiar to him.[14] But she overlooks Daniel, who provides as many instances as the fifty-nine she finds in Shakespeare. Tillyard also notes the great prominence Shakespeare gives to rebellion by his employment of the figure.[15] In Daniel this usage is in even greater concentration; we see the different aspects of a river in flood; the overbearing, raging current of the river and the obvious analogy to the surging psychological currents in man. This figure is most prominent in the *Civil Wars,* where it is closely related to the theme and structure of the whole.

Daniel adapts the epic simile to one form more than any other in the *Civil Wars,* particularly in those portions of earlier date—the figure of flowing rivers, of water filling up wide spaces, of inundation. The sense of the continuous flow of time is enhanced, as well as struggle, turbulence, even revolution; but generally what is suggested is smoothness and repose. At the outset, Rome's arduous origins are likened to the Rhine struggling and pushing its way in the long journey out of the mountains.[16] In another passage the powerful are shown flocking to join the usurping Bolingbroke, who will take their all but give little in thankful return; so the metaphor of the river makes vivid the action:

> And looke, how *Thames,* inricht with many a Flood,
> And goodly Rivers (that have made their Graves,
> And buried both their names and all their good
> Within his greatnes, to augment his waves)
> Glides on with pompe of Waters, unwithstood,
> Unto the *Ocean* (which his tribute craves)
> And layes up all his wealth, within that powre,
> Which in it selfe all greatnes doth devowre.   (II.7)

In the political context of this passage "Thames" is exactly the right choice, and "Ocean" carries the suggestion of death and oblivion that makes even royal greatness seem small. Wordsworth thought so much of these lines that one of his sonnets bears the quoted phrase "with pomp of waters, unwithstood." [17] Again, Henry IV's effort to check the rebellious discontent of his subjects is seen as a vain effort to arrest a flood: "Whil'st th'undersearching water, working-on,/Beares (proudly) downe, all that was idly don" (III.4).

Water imagery abounds in the *Civil Wars*. The alternating fortunes of France and England find expression in a simile of the tides (V.44), and the descendants of the Neville family are seen as "the spreading members of proud Po"—the metaphor of the river running on through a whole stanza (V.14 in early editions). Talbot, in a great passage (VI.93), fights manfully against the swelling stream and strong current of his French foes. And, again, the Duke of York's power is compared to proud Severn (VI.107), swollen with its tributaries, as it hurries on with its riches to the sea. In this passage, as in the stanza on Bolingbroke quoted above, the metaphorical function of the sea just emerges, but does so with ominous and ironic suggestion. These water-figures are prominent also in the Nile imagery of *Cleopatra;* are occasional in *Delia*, notably in the first sonnet; and are given extended treatment in at least two passages in *Musophilus* (271–86 and 927–30). In the longer *Musophilus* passage, the "humorous world" is likened to water wandering aimlessly from one empty river bed to another.

The other dominant metaphor, that of the house or building with its component rooms, though it is found in the early works, takes on increasing importance in the ethical poetry of 1599 and after. It becomes even more pervasive now than the water figure had been. Since Daniel so often in these poems is concerned with themes involving the permanence of moral and spiritual values in a world of flux, he is seeking for a symbol of stability—the well-built mind—as an edifice against the whimsical, unpredictable onslaught of ignorance, opinion, the mob, time itself. For a poet imbued with so much of stoicism, a better underlying metaphorical structure would be hard to find.

The building is a symbol of Musophilus' whole scale of values, and he reverts to it many times in his debate with Philocosmus. He finds, as has already been stated, in Stonehenge a symbol of building wrongly upon ignorance and material considerations. A weak foundation of blood and wrong produces too a weak edifice, even though it be a church; for "rage spar'd not the walls of pietie" (117–28). The ambitious can never find enough "rooms" because of their perpetual dissatisfaction (455).

No poem of Daniel's more fully develops the building metaphor than the epistle *To the Lady Margaret*, and the discussion of this work in Chapter Five makes the point clear. The mansion of virtue, a stronghold into which neither Fear nor Hope can enter to dismay the truly philosophical man, provides a lofty eminence from which he sees the vanity of things and recognizes what a glorious mansion he occupies. And the poems to Lady Lucy and Anne Clifford, as has been shown, abundantly give evidence of the same imagery. The picture that emerges, after a reading of the *Funeral Poem*, is that Devonshire has built well and that the poet has given him an appropriate room in a building, Daniel's own, that will stand. The poems on Sir Thomas Bodley and on Montaigne, concerned as they are with books and the transcendence of mind, express this same assurance that a place, a room, an edifice has been earned for them.

Like his contemporaries Daniel employs Classical myth as a metaphorical aid. The difference is that his use of it is sparing, and it is never a mere decorative excrescence but a well-integrated part of the whole. Even the Nemesis-Pandora myth in Book VI of the *Civil Wars*, a device to explain the origin of the modern gifts of grief, is a structural component and not a digression as some readers have supposed. This quiet assimilation of myth into the total fabric is evident in the Actaeon allusions of the fifth sonnet or in the casket episode in *Rosamond*. Drayton's *Mortimeriados*, with its profusion of mythological reference, placed alongside the *Civil Wars* illustrates Daniel's sparing and unostentatious use of such machinery. Proper names are frequently absent in Daniel's use of familiar myths, as in the ninth sonnet in which Sisyphus is not named but is clearly indicated in the line, "The never-resting stone of care to roule." The Actaeon story is similarly recalled by Montanus' speech in *Hymen's Triumph:*

> What pleasure can I take to chase wild beasts,
> When I my selfe am chac'd more egarly
> By mine owne passions, and can find no rest?
> Let them who have their heart at libertie,
> Attend those sports. I cannot be from hence,
> Where I receiv'd my hurt; here must I tread
> The maze of my perplexed miserie.   (688–94)

It is not that this assimilation of myth is not found in other poets, but that it is more regular in Daniel and bears significantly upon his development as a poet. The tendency to transform myth into metaphor may be seen as an earlier stage in the poet's shift from metaphor to abstraction, and therefore as symptomatic of his general movement away from sense-objects to conceptual thought.

In certain of the aspects of style discussed above the poet who later bears most resemblance to Daniel is Wordsworth. Coleridge noted in Chapter twenty-two of *Biographia Literaria* how in diction and ideas Wordsworth strikingly resembles Daniel, "one of the golden writers of our golden Elizabethan age." Wordsworth's own writings show this admiration for the earlier poet. In a letter of 1811 he acknowledges that one of his lines is taken directly from *Musophilus,* and he particularly recommends the epistle *To the Lady Margaret* for its meditative morality, its affecting dignity, and its applicability to Wordsworth's own times.[18] We find Wordsworth making annotations in a volume of Daniel, marking passages which he later assimilated into his own *Tintern Abbey* and *The Excursion,* and noting that the lines from the epistle to the Countess of Cumberland which he himself later used—"And that unlesse above himself he can/Erect himselfe, how poore a thing is man"—are a translation from Seneca. For one of his River Duddon sonnets (Number XVIII) he takes a line from *Musophilus* (295) and develops the octave of this sonnet with exactly the same rhymes as those in Daniel's stanza.

Wordsworth's "Character of the Happy Warrior," with its strong tone of Stoic fortitude, shows a careful reading of Daniel's *Funeral Poem* and of his epistle to Southampton. The introspection and melancholy in both poets is often revealed in their choice of diction.[19]

In the more indefinable realm of spirit the two poets are very much alike. Daniel perhaps more than Wordsworth speaks often of his hopes, his disappointments, his fear of having been born too late; and we are made to feel that he is a poet dedicated to a high purpose that is somehow never quite realized. Between the two poets is a common area of moral and spiritual autobiography. Both have been accused of talking too much about themselves, and often in a prosy manner. In Daniel, we sense a quiet central peace holding firm against a turbulent discordant world, and Wordsworth often resembles him. The kinship is at bottom moral. And long before Wordsworth, Daniel was touched by "the still sad music of humanity."

IV *The Sense of History*

The idea central to Daniel's view of the world is the acceptance of cyclical recurrence in human events. About this notion of alternating progress and decay he is more articulate than any other English poet of his time. And this basic assumption illuminates many of his characteristic ideas and attitudes. But recurrence in history, a familiar theme in Classical literature, goes back as far as Hesiod and Heraclitus. In Plato's *Statesman* the cycle of good and evil is seen as a process in which God must intervene to set the universe on its right course. Virgil's Fourth Eclogue envisions a cycle of history, and the Stoics recognize that recurrence must bring evil too. If the evil of the past must accompany the good, then the new is but a repetition of the old; and there is really no progress. And Daniel at times reflects this pessimism, one he no doubt imbibed in part from Marcus Aurelius and from Seneca.

In his own century two prominent French historiographers, while perhaps recognizing the pessimistic implications of the cyclical view, nevertheless used it as a framework for a more progressive, optimistic interpretation. Jean Bodin, whose work Daniel may well have known, wrote a widely read book that went through thirteen Latin editions between 1566 and 1650.[20] He forcefully rejects the Renaissance commonplace that man has degenerated from a golden age. For him history is shaped by man's changing will, and he sees a gradual ascent accompanying the rise and fall of cultures. He also contends for the excellence of modern achievement alongside the ancient, and in this respect he anticipates similar views by Daniel, especially in the *Defence*.

Louis Le Roy, a humanist and a student of Plato, published in 1577 his *De la vicissitude des choses en l'univers* that was translated into English in 1594 by Robert Ashley, Daniel's former school fellow at Magdalen College. For Le Roy, the universe is subject to corruption; and only divine intervention can renew it and revive the cycle. He discerns cyclical recurrence everywhere in the past; God grants excellence in the arts now to this people and now to that "that none should waxe proude by overlong prosperitie." [21] This concept, as will be seen later, is a theme reiterated in *Cleopatra* (1594). Despite the inevitable cycles, Le Roy sees a slow, steady growth in man's knowledge; and, like Bodin (and Daniel), he compares moderns with ancients in most favorable terms: the ancients haven't said all; there is much yet to be known; nature will again produce notable persons; men are made of the same stuff as before, and so on.

Daniel expresses these attitudes on many occasions. Perhaps his most extended account of historical cycles, occurring in *Cleopatra,* goes back to the Platonic doctrine. Important ideas on the nature of tragedy, as seen in the interplay between fate and character, are related here to the doctrine of recurrence. The philosophers Philosotratus and Arius are lamenting the destruction that has come to Egypt through luxury and impiety; then Arius speaks:

> O thou and I have heard, and read, and knowne
> Of like proude states, as wofully incombred,
> And fram'd by them, examples for our owne:
> Which now among examples must be numbred.
> For this decree a law from high is given,
> And ancient Canon, of eternall date,
> In Consistory of the starres of heaven,
> Entred the Booke of unavoyded Fate;
> That no state can in height of happinesse,
> In th'exaltation of their glory stand:
> But thither once arriv'd, declining lesse,
> Ruine themselves, or fall by others hand.
> Thus doth the ever-changing course of things
> Runne a perpetuall circle, ever turning:
> And that same day that hiest glory brings,
> Brings us unto the point of backe-returning.
> For sencelesse sensuality, doth ever
> Accompany felicity and greatnesse.

[171]

A fatall witch, whose charmes do leave us never,
Till we leave all in sorrow for our sweetnesse;
When yet our selves must be the cause we fall,
Although the same be first decreed on hie:
Our errors still must beare the blame of all
This must it be; earth, aske not heaven why.   (543–66)

The perpetual cycle is decreed; the downward turn, as in Plato, proceeds from the flaw of sensuality, Hamlet's "dram of eale." It is a fatal defect in human nature and its origin is a mystery—as is the identity, the oneness, of fate and character.

The very nature of the subject of the *Civil Wars*, the alternating fortunes of the two rival houses, lends itself to the idea of cyclical change. Daniel's disapproving account of the Lancastrian usurpation in the earlier books gradually gives way to a more unfavorable view of the Yorkists in the later uprisings. It is as though Yorkist violence has in some measure mitigated Bolingbroke's sin. But the poem offers little theorizing on historical cycles, and that may be because the theme is so much a part of the poem that literal statement would be superfluous. The point made in Arius' speech—that we are the cause of our own fall, though the fall is so decreed that it is vain to question heaven—is greatly elaborated on an individual level by Daniel in his presentation of Bolingbroke. To the end, the poet is uncertain about fixing the responsibility for evil-doing.

The idea of perpetual change, with nothing new emerging from the cycle, is found through almost all of Daniel's writings. It is succinctly expressed in the verse dedication to *Philotas* (26–30), and in his 1605 letter to Lord Cranborne, in which he alludes to human affairs "which in all ages beare the same resemblances, and are measured by one and the same foote of understanding. No tyme but brought forth the like concurrencies, the like interstriving for place and dignitie, the like supplantations, rysinges & overthrowes, so that there is nothing new under the Sunne, nothing in theas tymes that is not inn bookes, nor in bookes that is not in theas tymes." Similarly, in his prose dedication of the 1609 *Civil Wars* to the Countess of Pembroke, he reminds her that "Man is a creature of the same dimension he was: and how great and eminent soever hee bee, his measure and height is easie to be taken."

[172]

The idea is also set forth in considerable detail in the *Queenes Arcadia:*

> And have continued still the same and one
> In all successions from antiquitie;
> Whil'st all the states on earth besides have made
> A thousand revolutions, and have rowl'd
> From change to change, and never yet found rest,
> Nor ever bettered their estates by change. (2207–12)

Daniel's view of the Middle Ages is unusual for his time. That the world is not decaying is assurance that we are not the inferiors of the ancients. His deep respect for the Middle Ages has led one modern scholar to say that he "sometimes betrays a nostalgia for a world that has passed away" and that "he is one of the few Elizabethans to write of the Middle Ages with a sense of loss." [22] But he is not attracted to the strange marvels of medieval romance ("Let others sing of Knights and Palladines") but to the substance of the Middle Ages—its historical matter. There are many instances of this: the long list of medieval philosophers and historians in the *Defence* and in the prose *History,* the speech made to the poet by the spirit of Henry V in the *Civil Wars,* the poet's flattering description in Book VI of the *Civil Wars* of the peace and calm that blessed medieval Europe before the invention of printing and gunpowder, and the tribute paid to Chaucer in *Musophilus.*

Daniel's most memorable treatment of the Middle Ages is found in the *Defence,* which develops several implications of the belief in cyclical recurrence, one of the germinal ideas in the essay. If change and alteration go on forever and present recurring patterns, there is no "best." If man is ever the same—a Classical notion—there is no compelling reason for supposing the ancients our superiors. We are not to build by the square of Greece and Rome; medieval literature takes honorable rank with that which had gone before it. Daniel joins company with Sidney in laying the foundations of English criticism, which looks at its own national literature as worthy of study. There is neither unending progress nor gradual decay. The excellence of all ages and of all nations is assured by the revolution of time: "The distribution of giftes are universall, and all seasons hath them in some sort. We must not thinke, but that there were *Scipios, Caesars, Catoes,* and *Pompeies,* borne elsewhere then at *Rome,* the rest of the world hath ever had them in the same degree of nature, though not of state. And it is our weaknesse that makes us mistake, or misconceive in these deliniations of men the true figure of their worth." [23]

The awareness of the great truth that artistic excellence in every nation has its flowering season is asserted in Daniel's many tributes to his native literature and in his reasserted faith in the future of the English tongue. We can parallel Rome in every way; "Our Phoebus is the same that theirs hath beene"; "they cannot shew a *Sidney,*" whatever choice pieces they offer; Sidney has "th' Olimpian prize" and he "is not our all, although our best." [24]

In his *Defence* Daniel asserts that the different conceptions of wisdom and excellence in the world are but one, "apparelled according to the fashion of every nation." This notion of identity in the midst of diversity reveals a mind profoundly moved by a vision of history. In the historical process all matters of whatever importance will pass away—even Campion's quarrel with rhyme, as Daniel asserts in his closing sentence: "But this is but a Character of that perpetuall revolution that wee see to be in all things that never remaine the same, and we must herein be content to submit our selves to the law of time, which in a few yeares wil make al that, for which we now contend, *Nothing.*" [25] Gregory Smith calls the *Defence* "the flower of Elizabethan criticism," and he says that this final statement "is, as it were, the exaltation of fate and the refutation of finality in art." [26]

Throughout the *Defence* runs this theme of the law of time, with its fatal revolution of events and its superiority over the fixed judgment of an age. One feels that Daniel's perceptions as a critic grow out of a view of human history in which he sees all things undergoing perpetual change and yet, in the larger pattern of recurrence, remaining permanent. From this vantage point he is able to see literary canons as perpetually changing fashions, while at the same time the excellence of man's performance, or at least man's potential, is about the same in all ages.

V *Conclusion*

In both range and originality Daniel's contribution to English literature was large. He was either the first or among the first to establish in England the vogue of the sonnet, the moral verse-essay, the English historical verse-epic, the French-Senecan tragedy, the Italian pastoral drama, and the masque. He led the way in giving new life to the "mirror" poem through fusion with elements of the sonnet and the amatory poem. The union of elegy, epic, and "character" in the *Funeral Poem* was a unique achievement. Further testimonials of Daniel's literary versatility and scholarship are his translations from the Italian, his masterpiece in criticism, the *Defence,* and his prose *History*. He exercised a shaping influence on such contemporaries as Shakespeare and Drayton and later affected the poetry of Wordsworth.

Daniel's thought and art are consistent. At the center of all his work lies the Renaissance conviction of the superiority of man's moral and intellectual being over the mere things of this world, and over time itself. Conservative by nature, he sees man's excellence as enduring and as not determined merely by time and chance. He is as much a champion of culture and of "sweetness and light" as Matthew Arnold was to be three centuries later. He is never quaint, and there is always a modernity about him. For C. S. Lewis, Daniel is "in the nineteenth-century sense of the word, a poet of ideas"; he "actually thinks in verse: thinks deeply, arduously; he can doubt and wrestle . . . he is the most interesting man of letters of his century." [27]

As a poet, Daniel's note is more in the pathetic and elegiac strain than in the tragic and comic. He can be deeply affecting in a quiet, unobtrusive way. Although he is not one of the Olympians, he is among the second order of the best English poets. His muted melody, not always sensed at first hearing, continues to reach the ear and the understanding.

Notes and References

Chapter One

1. Thomas Fuller, *The Worthies of England,* ed. John Freeman (London, 1952), p. 500.

2. Harry Sellers, "A Bibliography of the Works of Samuel Daniel, 1585–1623," *Oxford Bibliographical Society Proceedings and Papers,* II (1927), 49. See also *Alumni Oxonienses,* which gives the matriculation date as November 17. Sellers gives as November 29, 1581, the date for Daniel's autograph signature in Oxford University Subscription Book Ab.

3. John Buxton, *Sir Philip Sidney and the English Renaissance* (London, 1954), pp. 161, 165.

4. *Ibid.,* pp. 148–50.

5. *Complete Works in Verse and Prose,* ed. Alexander B. Grosart, 5 vols. (Spenser Society, 1885–96), IV, 24–25. References to the text of Daniel's works, unless otherwise noted, are to this edition.

6. Grosart, IV, 6–7, 13. Joan Rees, in *Samuel Daniel: A Critical and Biographical Study* (Liverpool, 1964), p. 16, shows that quite likely "NW" was Nathaniel Webbe, an Oxford contemporary of Daniel's.

7. Mark Eccles, "Samuel Daniel in France and Italy," *Studies in Philology,* XXXIV (1937), 148–67.

8. Grosart, IV, 75.

9. This passage is pointed out as possibly supplying corroboration for Daniel's Italian journey by Laurence Michel in his edition of the *Civil Wars* (New Haven, 1958), p. 354. All subsequent references to the *Civil Wars,* unless otherwise noted, are to Michel's text.

10. The text for this and all subsequent references to Daniel's sonnets is *Poems and a Defence of Ryme,* ed. Arthur Colby Sprague (Cambridge, Mass., 1930).

11. A most delightful account is given by Leslie Hotson in his "Marigold of the Poets," *Transactions of the Royal Society of Literature of the United Kingdom,* XVII (London, 1938), 47–68. I have drawn upon Mr. Hotson's ingenious and, to me, convincing reconstruction of events at Lincoln.

12. Norreys J. O'Conor, *Godes Peace and the Queenes* (London, 1934), pp. 124–25.

13. John Florio, *Second Frutes* (London, 1591), pp. 79, 81.

14. John Aubrey, *Brief Lives,* ed. Andrew Clark (Oxford, 1898), 2 vols., I, 310–13.

15. Buxton, pp. 188–89.

16. Sprague, p. 129.

17. Grosart, in his edition of *The Complete Poems of Sir Philip Sidney* (London, 1877), III, 77, says that the countess' portion of the Psalms is "in advance of her brother's in thought, epithet, and melody" and that "her most remarkable poetry is found in these Psalms." Buxton (*Sir Philip Sidney,* p. 154) more modestly states that most readers have agreed that Lady Pembroke's Psalms "surpass her brother's." The whole of the one hundred and fifty Psalms were not published until 1823. More recently John Rathmell has edited and published all of the Psalms, from a collation of all the available manuscripts, in *The Psalms of Sir Philip Sidney and The Countess of Pembroke* (New York, 1963) in a Doubleday Anchor paperback.

18. *The Poems of Sir Philip Sidney,* ed. William A. Ringler (Oxford, 1962), p. 501.

19. Coleridge has a marginal comment on "To the Angell spirit" in a 1718 edition of Daniel: "This seems written *by,* or *for,* the Countess of Pembroke, Sister to Sir P. Sidney, who joined with him in the Psalms." See my "Coleridge Marginalia in Lamb's Copy of Daniel's *Poetical Works,*" *Harvard Library Bulletin,* VII (1953), 112.

20. Ringler, p. 509.

Chapter Two

1. Sprague, p. 9.

2. Of the several studies of foreign influence on Daniel's sonnets, perhaps the most useful discussion and summary is George Keyports Brady's *Samuel Daniel: a Critical Study* (Urbana, Illinois, 1923).

3. Grosart, I, xviii.

4. *Ibid.,* III, 23.

5. For the text of the Drayton poems, see Drayton's *Works,* ed. J. William Hebel, Katherine Tillotson, and Bernard H. Newdigate, 5 vols. (Oxford, 1931–41), Vol I. For commentary by the editors, see V, 13–15.

6. Claes Schaar, "An Elizabethan Sonnet Problem: Shakespeare's Sonnets, Daniel's Delia, and their Literary Background," *Lund Studies in English* (Copenhagen), XXVIII (1960), 1–190.

7. By Malone in 1780, and later Alden, J. Q. Adams, and Janet Scott. For a good summary of the question, see Hyder E. Rollins, ed.,

The Sonnets, by Shakespeare. New Variorum Edition (Philadelphia, 1944), 2 vols., II, 117–19.

8. All these resemblances and still others are recorded in their proper places by Rollins.

9. Janet Scott, *Les Sonnets élisabéthains* (Paris, 1929), pp. 248–50.

10. J. Q. Adams, *A Life of William Shakespeare* (Boston, 1923), pp. 169–70.

11. These contributions to the narrative by Daniel are pointed out by Virgil B. Heltzel in *Fair Rosamond,* Northwestern University Studies in the Humanities, XVI (Evanston, 1947), pp. 18–19.

12. This feature of the story is treated by Katherine Tillotson in Hebel's edition of Drayton, V, 102.

13. Willard Farnham, *The Medieval Heritage of Elizabethan Tragedy* (Berkeley, California, 1926), p. 321.

14. Another vision poem before *Rosamond* that gets told without resorting to a framework forced to support improbable fact is Thomas Lodge's *Scillaes Metamorphosis* (1589), a mythological tale thought to have influenced portions of Shakespeare's *Venus and Adonis.* It opens with the weeping poet's walking alone near the river Isis, where he meets the sea-god Glaucus, son of Thetis, who stills the poet's grief with an account of his own greater sorrow. The poet then actually witnesses the rest of the action, including the metamorphosis of Scylla, without having to rationalize the probability of what he relates.

15. For a fuller examination of these resemblances between *Rosamond* and related poems discussed here, see my "Daniel's *Complaint of Rosamond:* Origins and Influence of an Elizabethan Poem," *Lock Haven Bulletin,* I (1960), 47–56. There is additional discussion concerning the Drayton poems in the Hebel edition, Vol. V.

16. See Wilhelm Ewig, "Shakespeare and Daniel's *Complaint of Rosamond,*" Anglia, XXII (1899), 436–48, H. R. D. Anders, *Shakespeare's Books* (Berlin, 1904), pp. 85–89, and Sir Sidney Lee's introduction to his facsimile of *Lucrece* (Oxford, 1905), pp. 18–19. One must really examine these impressive lists of parallels to appreciate Shakespeare's probable debt to Daniel, not only in the sonnets, but in *Romeo and Juliet* as well.

17. The "hand" appears in lines 358, 370, 436, 437, 463, 467.

18. *Works of Thomas Nashe,* ed. Ronald B. McKerrow (London, 1904–10), I, 192.

19. From my "Wordsworth's Annotations in Daniel's *Poetical Works,*" *Modern Language Notes* (1953), pp. 403–6.

Chapter Three

1. On Senecan drama H. B. Charlton has a long and valuable study that appears as the "Introductory Essay on the Growth of the Senecan Tradition in Renaissance Tragedy" in *The Poetical Works of Sir William Alexander,* ed. L. E. Kastner and H. B. Charlton, 2 vols. (Manchester, 1921), Vol. 1. My discussion is guided mainly by this essay.

2. Lines 860–64 from *Antonie,* ed. Alice Luce (Weimar, 1897).

3. Representative of this general view is the commentary provided by A. M. Witherspoon in *The Influence of Robert Garnier on Elizabethan Drama* (New Haven, 1924), pp. 108–12.

4. For details of these resemblances, which are outside the scope of this chapter, the following discussions are useful: *The Tragedy of Antony and Cleopatra,* ed. R. H. Case (London, 1906), p. ix; New Variorum edition of *The Tragedy of Antony and Cleopatra,* ed. H. H. Furness (Philadelphia, 1907), pp. 514–15; Willard Farnham, *Shakespeare's Tragic Frontier* (Berkeley, California, 1950), pp. 165–74; Laurence Michel and Cecil C. Seronsy, "Shakespeare's History Plays and Daniel: An Assessment," *Studies in Philology,* LII (1955), 569–76; Arthur M. Z. Norman, "'The Tragedie of Cleopatra' and the Date of 'Antony and Cleopatra'," *Modern Language Review,* LIV (1959), 1–9.

5. For a detailed presentation of this view, see Michel and Seronsy, p. 574.

6. *Life of Sidney,* ed. Nowell Smith (Oxford, 1907), pp. 155–57.

7. *The Tragedy of Philotas,* ed. Laurence Michel (New Haven, 1949), pp. 155–56. All my references to the text of *Philotas* are to this edition.

8. The two letters are reprinted in Sellers, pp. 51–52.

9. Michel makes this point in *Philotas,* p. 43.

10. *Ibid.,* pp. 51–61.

11. *Ibid.,* p. 66.

Chapter Four

1. *Polimanteia* (London, 1595), Sigs. R2ᵛ–R3ʳ.

2. For a fuller discussion of these sources see Laurence Michel's Introduction to *The Civil Wars,* pp. 3–4. All references here to the text of this poem, unless otherwise specified, are to Michel's edition, although my readings came first from the original editions.

3. Grosart, III, 24.

4. The first of these two manuscripts antedating the 1595 printed version is British Museum Sloane 1443, first mentioned in Sellers *Bibliography,* p. 49, and then described and commented upon by me in "Daniel's Manuscript *Civil Wars* with Some Previously Unpublished

Stanzas," *Journal of English and Germanic Philology,* LII (1953), 153–60; and later by Michel in the Introduction to his edition of the *Civil Wars.* This is an early manuscript of the first two books. The other manuscript, Harleian 7332, appears to be the earliest version of Book III. For an account of this manuscript, see Cecil Seronsy and Robert Krueger, "A Manuscript of Daniel's *Civil Wars,* Book III, *Studies in Philology,* LXIII (1966), 157–62.

5. A detailed account of the parallels in treatment, situation, and language between Shakespeare's history plays and Daniel's *Civil Wars* is outside the scope of this discussion. A great number of such studies have been made, and they are summarized and added to by Michel and Seronsy in "Shakespeare's History Plays and Daniel"; and by Michel in his Introduction to the *Civil Wars,* pp. 7–28.

6. Sprague, p. 156.

7. E. M. W. Tillyard, *The English Epic and Its Background* (London, 1954), p. 322. The opening line of Daniel's poem "I sing the Civil Wars tumultuous strife" opens very much as Lucan's *Pharsalia* does, and Michel shows other similarities in temper between the two poets in his edition of the *Civil Wars.*

8. *Ibid.,* p. 325.

9. *Ibid.,* p. 332.

10. William Blissett, "Samuel Daniel's Sense of the Past," *English Studies,* XXXVIII (1957), 55.

11. *Works of Drayton,* ed. Hebel, V, 63–65.

Chapter Five

1. Sprague, pp. 156–57.

2. Frances A. Yates, *John Florio* (Cambridge, 1934), pp. 206–9.

3. *Ibid.,* pp. 196–97.

4. *The Vision of the Twelve Goddesses,* reprinted from the 1623 ed., with Introduction and Notes by Ernest Law (London, 1880), pp. 13–14.

5. British Museum Royal MS 17 B. XV. There are other flattering allusions to Daniel and his contemporaries in this fumbling poem.

6. Reprinted in part by H. Sellers in "Samuel Daniel: Additions to the Text," *Modern Language Review,* XI (1916), 28–32.

7. George C. Williamson, *Lady Anne Clifford, Countess of Dorset, Pembroke and Montgomery, 1590–1676: Her Life, Letters and Work* (Kendal, 1922), p. 63.

8. See Ruth Hughey's edition of *The Arundel Harington Manuscript of Tudor Poetry,* 2 vols. (Columbus, Ohio, 1960), I, 265–74, and Notes.

9. *Ibid.,* II, 372.

10. Martha Hale Shackford, "Samuel Daniel's Poetical *Epistles,* Especially that to the Countess of Cumberland," *Studies in Philology,* XLV (1948), 182–88.

11. These passages from the play and the letter are cited and quoted by Holger Norgaard in "Shakespeare and Daniel's 'Letter from Octavia'," *Notes and Queries,* CC (1955), 56–57. Norgaard, however, does not discuss Shakespeare's adaptation of the psychological mood in Daniel's suggestive treatment to other persons and situations suited to his own dramatic scheme.

12. Sprague, Introduction, pp. xx–xxi.

13. Grosart, IV, 7.

14. Raymond Himelick, "Samuel Daniel, Montaigne, and Seneca," *Notes and Queries,* III (1956), 61–64. Himelick, in the excellent Introduction to his recent edition of *Musophilus* (Purdue University Studies, 1965), pp. 40–43, discusses more fully the Stoic indoctrination of Daniel.

15. Raymond Himelick, "*A Fig for Momus* and Daniel's *Musophilus,*" *Modern Language Quarterly,* XVIII (1957), 247–50.

16. Sprague, 11. 995–1003. All references to the text of *Musophilus,* the *Epistles,* and the *Defence of Ryme* are to Sprague's edition.

17. Fulke Greville, *Poems and Dramas,* ed. Geoffrey Bullough, 2 vols. (New York, 1945), I, st. 75.

18. Bullough, I, 53–54.

19. Sprague, p. 156.

20. By Sellers. See note 6 above.

21. Seneca, *Moral Essays,* trans. John W. Basore, 3 vols. (London, 1928–1935), III, 4.

22. Shackford, p. 182.

23. *Thomas Campion,* ed. A. H. Bullen (London, 1903), pp. 235–67.

24. Sprague, p. 131.

25. *Ibid.,* pp. 139–40.

26. *Ibid.,* p. 143.

Chapter Six

1. Since the original autograph of this letter has not been found, modern scholars are inclined to question the authenticity of the printed transcriptions of it and even to suspect it as a forgery. (See Sprague, Introduction, p. xviii.) Because the contents of the letter afford valuable information, it is important at this point that the evidence supporting its authenticity be given.

When Sir Egerton Brydges published the letter in *Censura Literaria* in 1808 (VI.391–93) and later in 1815 (VI.128–30), he said that his transcribed copy came from the descendant of the Lord Keeper, Francis Henry Egerton, who was then in the process of writing a "Life" of his ancestor, though it had not yet been published. It was upon this transcription that all the later printings were based, and it has been wrongly assumed that Francis Henry Egerton never printed the letter. He did print it; his *Life*, privately printed in 1798 and 1801, contains the text of the letter and evidently Brydges never saw this book. There seems to be no compelling reason for questioning the sincerity of Francis Henry Egerton's transcription. Furthermore, Daniel's gift copy of the *Works*, now in Huntington Library, has the remains of a broken seal on the inside of the cover, suggesting an attached enclosure. (See Virgil B. Heltzel, "Sir Thomas Egerton as Patron," *Huntington Library Quarterly*, XI [1948], 116.) The old bogey of a John Payne Collier forgery has also been raised; but, unfortunately for this view, Collier could have been only nine years old at the time Egerton published the *Life*.

For fuller details see my article "The Case for Daniel's Letter to Egerton Reopened," *The Huntington Library Quarterly*, XXIX (November, 1965), 79–82.

2. Francis Henry Egerton, *The Life of Sir Thomas Egerton* (London: published March 1, 1798, by S. Harding), p. 57. Grosart (I, 10–11) also prints the full text of this letter.

3. Grosart, I, 4–7. For this and other occasional poems quoted here, references are to the page numbers in Grosart.

4. *Ibid.*, I, 280.

5. *Ibid.*, I, 290–93.

6. *England's Mourning Garment*, London [1603], Sig. D2^{v}.

7. See Buxton, p. 228.

8. British Museum Royal MS 18A LXXII.

9. Seller's *Bibliography*, p. 49. I have examined the manuscript and agree with Sellers.

10. The quoted text of this poem is from Grosart, I, 143–67.

11. A. L. Rowse, *Ralegh and the Throckmortons* (London, 1962), p. 233.

12. Ralegh's use of the Daniel passage is cited by Peter Ure in "Two Elizabethan Poets: Daniel and Ralegh," *Guide to English Literature* (1956), II, 123–38. Ure points out additionally that the quoted lines are very pertinent to Ralegh's own situation and that Daniel was "almost the only contemporary English poet honoured by quotation in Ralegh's vast book."

13. *The Letters and Epigrams of Sir John Harington, together with the Prayse of Private Life*, ed. Norman E. McClure (Philadelphia, 1930), Epigram 340.

14. For a discussion of the relationship with Hertford and the probable date of the association, see my "Daniel's Panegyrike and the Earl of Hertford," *Philological Quarterly*, XXXII (1953), 342–44; and Joan Rees, "Samuel Daniel and the Earl of Hertford," *Notes and Queries*, CCIII (1958), 408.

15. E. K. Chambers, *The Elizabethan Stage*, 4 vols. (Oxford, 1923), III, 280.

16. Law, *Vision of the Twelve Goddesses*, pp. 10–11.

17. *Ibid.*, p. 13.

18. Grosart, III, 187.

19. *Ibid.*, III, 195.

20. *Ibid.*, III, 193–94.

21. Enid Welsford, *The Court Masque* (Cambridge, 1927), p. 173.

22. See Adams, *A Life of William Shakespeare*, p. 359.

23. Chambers, III, 49–51.

24. See R. E. Brettle, "Samuel Daniel and the Children of the Queen's Revels, 1604–5," *Review of English Studies*, III (1927), 162–68.

25. All quotations from the poem are from the Sprague edition, pp. 161–63.

26. Douglas Bush, *Mythology and the Renaissance Tradition in English Poetry* (Minneapolis, Minn., 1932), p. 219.

27. A. E. Housman, *The Name and Nature of Poetry* (New York, 1933), p. 7.

28. Sellers, p. 47.

29. Buxton, p. 225.

30. *Letters and Epigrams*, pp. 323–78. The text is printed from the British Museum Additional MS 30161, itself a transcript made from a still earlier MS, now at Appleby Castle, by William Ford (1771–1832). Ford ascribes it to Harington but adds, "Upon a blank leaf, prefixed, was written 'For the Countesse Dowager of Comberland, presented by Samuel Daniell'." This leaf, says Sellers ("Supplementary Note to a Bibliography of the Works of Samuel Daniel," *Oxford Bibliographical Society Proceedings and Papers*, II [1930], pp. 341–42), has disappeared, with some others, from the original MS, which he finds written in ordinary copyist's hand of the period. The ascription to Harington depends on the fact that the word "Harrington" (also a Cumberland place name) appears at the extreme top of an otherwise blank preliminary leaf of paper different from the MS, with which it has apparently no connection. Sellers is correct in regarding these facts as slim evidence for Harington's authorship.

31. Ed. Archibold Davison and Willi Appel (Cambridge, Mass., 1947), pp. 184, 235.

32. Sellers' *Bibliography*, p. 39.

33. William Camden, *Remaines of a Greater Worke* (London, 1605).

34. Robert Naunton, *Fragmenta Regalia* (London, 1641), p. 42. This work and the following are the principal sources for my account of Mountjoy: various biographies by Sir Sidney Lee in the *Dictionary of National Biography*; Fynes Moryson, *An Itinerary* (1617), 4 vols. (Glasgow, 1907–1908); James Spedding, ed., *The Works of Francis Bacon* (London, 1862), Vol. II; *Calendar of State Papers, Domestic* (Reigns of Elizabeth and James I); Cyril Falls, *Mountjoy: Elizabethan General* (London, 1955).

35. *Itinerary*, II, 260.

36. The text of the poem cited here is that of the second and expanded edition, *A Funerall Poem Uppon the Death of the Late noble Earle of Devonshyre* (London, 1607). No modern edition of the poem is available except Grosart's, which is careless and inaccurate. For example, Grosart at times prints both original and revised versions of passages and thus makes Daniel appear to be repeating himself in almost identical language.

Chapter Seven

1. Walter W. Greg, *Pastoral Poetry and Pastoral Drama* (London, 1906), p. 261.

2. *The Letters of John Chamberlain*, ed. Norman E. McClure, 2 vols. (Philadelphia, 1939), I, 208.

3. *Ibid.*, I, 504, 507.

4. Greg, p. 252, shows this in great detail. V. M. Jeff'rey, in "Italian and English Pastoral Drama of the Renaissance," *Modern Language Review*, XIX (1924), 435–40, sees the whole play as "a jumble of borrowed episodes, strung together by melodious verse," although Daniel's method of borrowing is seen as precise and deliberate. The Italian sources are here shown to be Tasso, Guarini, and Groto.

5. Grosart, III, 1150–56, 1159–64. All quoted passages in this chapter from the masques and pastoral drama are from Grosart's text.

6. Kenneth Muir, in *Shakespeare's Sources*, I (London, 1957), p. 167, mentions some of the resemblances. In "Shakespeare and Daniel: More Echoes," *Notes and Queries*, CCV (1960), 328–29, I have cited additional parallels.

7. Grosart, III, 311–16.

8. Percy Simpson and C. F. Bell, *Designs by Inigo Jones For Masques and Plays at Court* (Oxford, 1924), p. 43.

9. Welsford, pp. 188–89.

10. *Correspondence of Sir Robert Kerr, First Earl of Ancrum and*

His Son William, Third Earl of Lothian, ed. David Laing (Edinburgh, 1875), 2 vols., Introduction, I, viii.

11. The manuscript is part of the Drummond of Hawthornden collection there. Since several of the songs of the printed version are not in the manuscript, we may infer that the manuscript is an earlier version and that Daniel wrote the play with no specific occasion in mind.

12. Reprinted in Grosart, IV, lvi.

13. *Pastoral Poetry and Pastoral Drama,* p. 256.

Chapter Eight

1. For this preface see Sprague, pp. 3–5.

2. Gerald Langbaine, *An Account of the English Dramatick Poets* (Oxford, 1691), p. 100.

3. These letters were first printed by Sellers in his *Bibliography,* pp. 52–53, and the Oxford Bibliographical Society has given me permission to quote from them. I have expanded all obvious abbreviations.

4. The fact of Hertford's residence is established by *Letters of Chamberlain,* II, 364; and *Calendar of State Papers, Domestic, James I* [1611–1618], p. 92.

5. *Calendar of State Papers, Domestic, James I* [1603–1610], p. 126.

6. *Ibid.,* 1580–1625, Addenda, p. 515.

7. Grosart IV, 79–80. All references to the prose *History* and the *Collection* are to the Grosart text by volume and page number.

8. Michel, *Civil Wars,* pp. 68–69.

9. William L. Godshalk, "Daniel's *History,*" *Journal of English and Germanic Philology,* LXIII (1964), p. 53.

10. Daniel's use of sources is traced in considerable detail by Godshalk, pp. 54–56.

11. Rudolf B. Gottfried, "Samuel Daniel's Method of Writing History," *Studies in the Renaissance,* III (1956), 157–74.

12. Godshalk, pp. 45–50, and Gottfried, "The Authorship of *A Breviary of the History of England,*" *Studies in Philology,* LIII (1956), 172–90.

13. Gottfried, "The Authorship of *A Breviary,*" p. 184.

14. *Calendar of State Papers, Domestic, James I,* [1611–1618], pp. 294, 549.

15. *Ibid.,* p. 357.

16. Yates, *John Florio,* pp. 249, 260.

17. Sellers, p. 50.

18. *Ibid.,* p. 50. Daniel's wife might have preceded him in death a short time before. Mrs. Hilda Massey, who has diligently searched through local records for me, reports that just before the burial entry

at Beckington for "Mr. Samuell Daniel" on 14 October, 1619, is an entry for 25 March 1618/19, which records the burial of a "Daniell," the name preceded by what appears to be a faint "Mrs."

Chapter Nine

1. *Runne and a Great Cast,* London [1614], Sig. I4ʳ.

2. The phrase from Browne occurs in *Britannia's Pastorals,* Book II, Song 2, 1. 303; Drummond of Hawthornden's remark may be found in *Critical Essays of the Seventeenth Century,* ed. Joel E. Spingarn, 3 vols. (Oxford, 1908–1909), I, 216; Spenser's lines are from *Colin Clouts Come Home Again,* 11. 416–27; the two Drayton judgments are from *Endimion and Phoebe,* 11. 997–1000 and "To Henry Reynolds of Poets and Poesy," 11. 123–28; Bolton's conclusion is in Spingarn, I, 10.

3. *The Athenaeum* (July 29, 1854), pp. 941–42. Gray's unpublished essay on Daniel was taken from his notes for what was said to be an intended history of English poetry.

4. *Coleridge's Literary Criticism,* ed. J. W. Mackail (London, 1921), pp. 119, 154, 64–65.

5. *English Epic and Heroic Poetry* (London, 1912), pp. 179–80, 187–88.

6. Texts of the *Civil Wars* referred to in this chapter are from the Michel edition unless otherwise specified. All references to the *Delia* sonnet sequence, *Rosamond, Musophilus,* the verse *Epistles,* and *Defence of Ryme* are to Sprague's edition. For *Philotas* the text cited is the edition by Michel. All other references are to Grosart.

7. In this passage Coleridge finds "a Pun in its right place and passion. Had Puns never been used less judiciously than in this Instance and that of the fallen Angels in the 6th Book of Paradise Lost, they would still have been considered as Beauties." See my article, "Coleridge Marginalia in Lamb's Copy of Daniel's *Poetical Works,*" *Harvard Library Bulletin,* VII (1953), 109.

8. *Coleridge's Literary Criticism,* p. 64.

9. Some idea of its frequency may be had from the following tabulation: it occurs as end-rhyme ten times in the sonnets, six times in *Rosamond,* eight times in *Cleopatra,* twenty-eight times in the *Civil Wars,* five times in *A Letter to Octavia,* twice in *Musophilus,* three times in the verse *Epistles,* five times in the *Panegyrike,* ten times in *Philotas,* thirteen times in the *Queenes Arcadia,* twice in the *Funeral Poem,* and six times in *Hymen's Triumph.* On this point, a comparison of the *Civil Wars* with Drayton's two epics of English history is again instructive. In the whole of *Mortimeriados,* totaling almost three thousand lines, "the same" does not once occur as an end-rhyme, while

only twice does it appear elsewhere in the line. In the still longer *Barons' Wars,* the expression occurs only once as end-rhyme and three times elsewhere in the line.

10. Laurence Michel first called attention to this habit of Daniel's in his edition of *Philotas,* pp. 30–33. Some of my examples were first cited by Michel.

11. Thomas M. Raysor, *Coleridge's Miscellaneous Criticism* (Cambridge, Mass., 1936), p. 238.

12. For these and other commentaries see my "Coleridge Marginalia," pp. 108–11.

13. *Poetic Imagery* (New York, 1924), pp. 30–31.

14. Caroline Spurgeon, *Shakespeare's Imagery* (New York, 1936), pp. 50, 93–96.

15. *Shakespeare's History Plays,* pp. 221–22.

16. I, 17 (in 1595 and 1599 editions only).

17. Wordsworth's *Poetical Works,* ed. Ernest de Selincourt and Helen Darbishire, 5 vols. (Oxford, 1940–1949), III, 117.

18. *The Letters of William and Dorothy Wordsworth, The Middle Years,* ed. Ernest de Selincourt, 6 vols. (Oxford, 1935–1939), II, 477.

19. Fuller discussion of these and other Daniel-Wordsworth relationships will be found in my "Daniel and Wordsworth," *Studies in Phililogy,* LVI (1959), 187–213.

20. *Method for the Easy Comprehension of History,* translated by Beatrice Reynolds (New York, 1945).

21. Robert Ashley, trans., *Of the Inter-changeable Course, or Variety of Things in the Whole World* (London, 1594), fol. 33ᵛ.

22. May McKisack, "Samuel Daniel as Historian," *Review of English Studies,* XXIII (1947), 238.

23. Sprague, pp. 143–44.

24. Dedicatory lines to the 1607 edition of *Cleopatra* (London), Sig. A4ʳ.

25. Sprague, p. 158.

26. George Gregory Smith, ed., *Elizabethan Critical Essays,* 2 vols. (Oxford, 1904), I, Introduction, lxiv.

27. C. S. Lewis, *English Literature in the Sixteenth Century* (Oxford, 1954), pp. 530–31.

Selected Bibliography

PRIMARY SOURCES

1. First and Early Editions

These are listed and described in the following bibliographies which are often necessary for consultation because modern editions are incomplete.

SELLERS, HARRY. "A Bibliography of the Works of Samuel Daniel, 1585–1623," *Oxford Bibliographical Society Proceedings and Papers* (Bodleian Library, Oxford), II (1927), 29–54. Contains a thoroughly reliable bibliographical description of all editions appearing in the author's lifetime with the additional posthumous one edited by his brother and published in 1623.

————. "Samuel Daniel: Additions to the Text," *Modern Language Review*, XI (1916), 28–32.

TANNENBAUM, SAMUEL A. *Samuel Daniel, A Concise Bibliography*. Elizabethan Bibliographies. New York: Samuel Aaron Tannenbaum, 1942. Provides a valuable listing of various textual, biographical, and critical writings on Daniel.

2. Modern Editions, Listed Chronologically

GROSART, ALEXANDER B., ed. *Complete Works in Verse and Prose*. London: Hazell, Watson and Viney, 1885–1896. 5 vols. The only full edition of Daniel's writings to date, the Grosart text is frequently untrustworthy; and, whenever possible, the more recent editions of individual works should be consulted, with their introductions and notes.

LEDERER, MAX, ed. *The Tragedy of Cleopatra* (1611 text). Louvain: University of Louvain, 1911.

SPRAGUE, ARTHUR COLBY, ed. *Poems and a Defence of Ryme*. Cambridge, Mass.: Harvard University Press, 1930.

MICHEL, LAURENCE, ed. *The Tragedy of Philotas*. New Haven: Yale University Press, 1949.

————, ed. *The Civil Wars*. New Haven: Yale University Press, 1958.

Selected Bibliography

HIMELICK, RAYMOND, ed. *Musophilus*. Purdue University Studies. Indianapolis, Indiana: C. E. Pauley and Company, 1965.

SECONDARY SOURCES

ALEXANDER, SIR WILLIAM. *Poetical Works*. Ed. L. E. Kastner and H. B. Charlton. 2 vols. Edinburgh: W. Blackwood and Sons, 1921. Vol. I. Introduction. Charlton's long essay on the development of various strains of Senecan drama is especially valuable to the student of the Garnier type of tragedy in England.

ANDERS, H. R. D. *Shakespeare's Books*. Berlin: G. Reimer, 1904. Offers numerous parallel passages, more or less convincing, between Daniel and Shakespeare to demonstrate principally the influence of *Rosamond* on *Lucrece* and on *Romeo and Juliet*.

BLISSETT, WILLIAM. "Samuel Daniel's Sense of the Past," *English Studies*, XXXVIII (1957), 49–63. Argues for Daniel's medievalism in its best sense—its thought and learning—and for his sense of the continuity of history.

BRADY, GEORGE KEYPORTS. *Samuel Daniel, A Critical Study*. Urbana: University of Illinois, 1923. The best presentation of evidence on the sources for Daniel's sonnets and their probable influence on other poets. Inferences are sensible and judgments are balanced.

BRETTLE, R. E. "Samuel Daniel and the Children of the Queen's Revels, 1604–5," *Review of English Studies*, III (April, 1927), 162–68. A discussion, based upon legal documents, that sheds some light on Daniel's activities during the period 1604–1609.

BUXTON, JOHN. *Sir Philip Sidney and the English Renaissance*. London: MacMillan and Company, 1954. An informative, sensitively written book on the Renaissance background of Sidney and the Wilton group of poets. Has extensive discussion of Daniel's poetry and his associations.

CAMPBELL, LILY B., ed. *The Mirror for Magistrates*. Cambridge: The University Press, 1938. The best edition of a book that is indispensable to an understanding of sixteenth-century concepts of history and tragedy and of *Rosamond* and its progeny.

DRAYTON, MICHAEL. *Works*. Ed. J. William Hebel, Katherine Tillotson, and Bernard H. Newdigate. 5 vols. Oxford: B. Blackwell, 1931–1941. The most reliable texts, together with valuable introductions and notes, to the many writings of Drayton that were more or less indebted to Daniel.

ECCLES, MARK. "Samuel Daniel in France and Italy," *Studies in Philology* (XXXIV), 148–67. Offers documentary evidence for Daniel's journeys abroad before 1590.

FULLER, THOMAS. *The History of the Worthies of England*. Ed. P.

Austin Nuttall. London: T. Tegg, 1840. 3 vols. An early biography of Daniel, brief, sprightly and witty; makes some claims of fact as yet unsubstantiated.

GODSHALK, WILLIAM L. "Daniel's *History*," *Journal of English and Germanic Philology*, LXIII (1964), 45–57. Argues, largely on basis of style, for Daniel's authorship of *A Breviary of the History of England* and demonstrates Daniel's originality in the use of his sources.

GOTTFRIED, RUDOLF B. "Samuel Daniel's Method of Writing History," *Studies in the Renaissance*, III (1956), 157–74. Shows in great detail how closely Daniel followed a French source for a part of his prose *History*, and yet how he is not a mere copyist but has "condensed, reorganized, and expanded this material with insertions out of other sources and reflections of his own."

————. "The Authorship of *A Breviary of the History of England*," *Studies in Philology*, LIII (1956), 172–90. Argues convincingly, on the basis of text and organization of materials, that Daniel, and not Ralegh, was the author of the *Breviary*, and suggests an early date for Daniel's beginning the prose *History*.

GREG, WALTER W. *Pastoral Poetry and Pastoral Drama*. London: A. H. Bullen, 1906. Shows how closely Daniel followed his Italian models but tends to exaggerate his slavishness in translation and to ignore his original contributions to plot.

GREVILLE, FULKE. *Poems and Dramas*. Ed. Geoffrey Bullough. 2 vols. Edinburgh: Oliver and Boyd, 1939. Best modern edition of the writings of a friend and patron of Daniel which at many points show an identity of ideas and interests with Daniel's work.

HELTZEL, VIRGIL B. *Fair Rosamond*. Northwestern University Studies in the Humanities, XVI. Evanston: Northwestern University Press, 1947. An interesting account of a historical character, with all its subsequent legendary and literary encrustations down to the present time. Specifies some of Daniel's contributions to the story.

HIMELICK, RAYMOND. "*A Fig for Momus* and Daniel's *Musophilus*," *Modern Language Quarterly*, XVIII (1957), 247–50. A neatly presented case for Lodge's poem as a likely suggestion to Daniel, who greatly enlarged upon the same theme and gave more emphasis to the humanist side of the argument.

HOTSON, LESLIE. "Marigold of the Poets," *Transactions of the Royal Society of Literature of the United Kingdom* (London, 1938), XVII, 47–68. Absorbing, charming reconstruction from official documents of some exciting events involving Daniel in the early 1590's.

HUGHEY, RUTH, ed. *The Arundel Harington Manuscript of Tudor Poetry*. 2 vols. Columbus, Ohio: Ohio State University Press, 1960. Contains an earlier manuscript version of *A Letter from Octavia*, together with some thoughtful discussion of its relation to the Countess of Cumberland and the Wilton circle.

MORYSON, FYNES. *An Itinerary*. 4 vols. Glasgow: J. MacLehose and Sons, 1907–1908. Recounts at various points the actions of Lord Mountjoy in the Irish campaign, and affords good background for a reading of the *Funeral Poem*, in which Daniel's fidelity to historical truth is made clear.

NORMAN, ARTHUR M. Z. "'The Tragedie of Cleopatra' and the Date of 'Antony and Cleopatra'," *Modern Language Review*, LIV (1959), 1–9. Argues that the evidence suggests an earlier date for Shakespeare's *Antony and Cleopatra* than for Daniel's important revision of *Cleopatra* in 1607, and that Shakespeare here influenced Daniel.

RAYSOR, THOMAS M. *Coleridge's Miscellaneous Criticism*. Cambridge, Mass.: Harvard University Press, 1936. Contains illuminating critical commentary by Coleridge on various aspects of Daniel as man and writer.

REES, JOAN. *Samuel Daniel, A Critical and Biographical Study*. Liverpool: Liverpool University Press, 1964. This, the first full-length study of Daniel, brings to light some of the poet's literary associations and offers valuable insights into Daniel's originality as a sonneteer.

ROLLINS, HYDER E., ed. *The Sonnets* by Shakespeare. New Variorum Edition. Philadelphia: Lippincott, 1944. A good documented summary of the arguments for and against Daniel's influence on Shakespeare's sonnets, with Rollins favoring the affirmative position.

SCHAAR, CLAES. "An Elizabethan Sonnet Problem: Shakespeare's Sonnets, Daniel's Delia, and their Literary Background," *Lund Studies in English* (Copenhagen, 1960), No. 28, pp. 1–190. Argues from exhaustive study of diction, grammar, rhetoric, and imagery, that there is no evidence for Daniel's influencing Shakespeare, but that the reverse is more likely. Tends to minimize evidence to the contrary, such as priority of dating for *Delia* and occasional patent identity of mood between the two sequences.

SCHÜTZE, JOHANNES. "Daniels 'Cleopatra' und Shakespeare," *Englische Studien*, LXXI (1936), 58–72. Argues strongly against Shakespeare's influencing Daniel in the 1607 edition of *Cleopatra*, since Daniel recast only the material from his earlier edition.

SCOTT, JANET G. *Les Sonnets élisabéthains*. Paris: Champion, 1929.

Discusses origins and influence of the *Delia* sonnets; suggests, by offering a number of parallel passages, that *Delia* afforded a model for Shakespeare.

SERONSY, CECIL. "Coleridge Marginalia in Lamb's Copy of Daniel's *Poetical Works*," *Harvard Library Bulletin*, VII (1953), 107–12. Valuable observations by Coleridge on various aspects of Daniel's art, particularly his versification in the *Civil Wars*. The commentary of Coleridge is, like that in the Raysor book, warmly appreciative.

————. "Well-Languaged Daniel Reconsidered," *Modern Language Review*, LII (1957), 481–97. A detailed study of the poet's diction, versification, and imagery that attempts to arrive at a precise understanding of his strength and weakness as a poet.

————. "The Doctrine of Cyclical Recurrence and Some Related Ideas in the Works of Samuel Daniel," *Studies in Philology*, LIV (1957), 387–407. An account of an idea central to Daniel's thought and its assimilation into the fabric of a large number of his works.

————. "Daniel and Wordsworth," *Studies in Philology*, LVI (1959), 187–213. Offers direct testimony from Wordsworth and numerous resemblances between the two poets in diction, imagery, and thought, as strongly suggesting that Wordsworth learned much from Daniel.

SHACKFORD, MARTHA HALE. "Samuel Daniel's *Poetical Epistles*, Especially that to the Countess of Cumberland," *Studies in Philology*, XLV (1948), 180–95. Emphasizes Daniel's strong sympathy for woman's point of view in the *Poetical Epistles*, as well as in *Rosamond*, *Cleopatra*, and *Octavia*. Demonstrates how the imagery is suitable to the subject.

TILLYARD, E. M. W. *Shakespeare's History Plays*. New York: The Mac-Millan Company, 1946. Discusses probable influence of the *Civil Wars* on Shakespeare; shows how both writers are identical in scope and political philosophy and very similar in choice of incidents.

————. *The English Epic and Its Background*. London: Chatto and Windus, 1954. Along with Michel's Introduction to the *Civil Wars*, the most reliable study of Daniel's narrative poem for its place in the epic tradition. Shows how Daniel's concern with the motives of political action and the dignity of his verse give his poem some share of epic quality, although it lacks "the amplitude and variety that mark the great epics."

WOOD, ANTHONY. *Athenae Oxonienses*. Ed. Philip Bliss. 4 vols. London: F. C. and J. Rivington, 1813. One of the earliest biographies of Daniel, which, though making some unsupported claims of fact, provides the basis for later biographical accounts.

YATES, FRANCES A. *John Florio.* Cambridge: The University Press, 1934. A very readable biography of Daniel's good friend that provides many items of information shedding light on Daniel's associations. From slender factual evidence, Yates sometimes draws inferences which later became assumptions for even more doubtful inferences.

Index